Managing
Motivation

Managing Motivation

A Manager's Guide to Diagnosing and Improving Motivation

Robert D. Pritchard

Elissa L. Ashwood

Routledge
Taylor & Francis Group
New York   London

Routledge
Taylor & Francis Group
270 Madison Avenue
New York, NY 10016

Routledge
Taylor & Francis Group
2 Park Square
Milton Park, Abingdon
Oxon OX14 4RN

© 2008 by Taylor & Francis Group, LLC
Routledge is an imprint of Taylor & Francis Group, an Informa business

Printed in the United States of America on acid-free paper
10 9 8 7 6 5 4 3 2 1

International Standard Book Number-13: 978-1-84169-789-5 (Softcover) 978-1-84169-713-0 (Hardcover)

Library of Congress Cataloging-in-Publication Data

Pritchard, Robert D.
    Managing motivation : a manager's guide to diagnosing and improving motivation / Robert Pritchard and Elissa Ashwood.
        p. cm.
    Includes bibliographical references and index.
    ISBN 978-1-84169-789-5 (alk. paper) -- ISBN 978-1-84169-713-0 (alk. paper) 1. Employee motivation. 2. Behavior modification. I. Ashwood, Elissa. II. Title.

HF5549.5.M63P75 2008
658.3'14--dc22   2008012575

Visit the Taylor & Francis Web site at
http://www.taylorandfrancis.com

and the Psychology Press Web site at
http://www.psypress.com

This book is dedicated to the manager who believes
that more is possible—and proves it.
Discovery consists of looking
at the same things as everyone else
and thinking something different.

—Albert Szent-Gyorgi

Contents

Chapter 6

Diagnosing Action-to-Results Connections 53

Chapter 7

Diagnosing Results-to-Evaluation Connections 69

Preface

Before getting into the content of this book, we wanted to tell you a bit about ourselves and why we wrote it.

Bob Pritchard is Professor of Organizational Psychology and Management at the University of Central Florida. He received his bachelor's degree from UCLA and his PhD from the University of Minnesota. He has been on the faculty of Purdue University, the University of Houston, and Texas A&M University. He has worked in the area of motivation and performance in organizations for more than 35 years and has published 7 books and more than 90 articles on the subject. His award-winning research program has developed techniques for improving motivation and organizational effectiveness that have been used by many organizations in the United States and in other countries.

Elissa Ashwood provides the practitioner's viewpoint. She holds an MBA in finance and accounting from the University of Rochester, and has served as a vice-president of accounting, director of leadership programs, and director of training and development for three Fortune 100 companies. She has consulted with top consulting and service firms in the areas of executive effectiveness, compensation, and performance and is committed to developing organizational strategies that help people to do their best work.

The idea for this book first came about while Bob was working with the top management team of Personnel Decisions, International to develop an organizational measurement and feedback system. The CFO at the time was Peter Ramstad, and the more Bob and Pete talked about this motivation approach, the more Pete convinced Bob that this work contained some important insights that would be of practical use to managers.

Bob started the book and Elissa joined the effort to use her extensive experience in management training to help make the book more usable for managers. One of the most enjoyable parts of this collaboration was our very different backgrounds, which led to some highly positive synergy.

We also share a number of important values that guided this book. We believe that while there is some good work being done in the academic setting, there are fewer attempts to translate that academic work into *practical* terms a manager can actually use. Without that translation, the academic work has less impact. We also believe that work done in management needs to be based on a strong conceptual foundation supported by good research. Most management books are either highly academic, and not particularly practical, or practically oriented but lack a strong conceptual and research foundation.

We decided that by working together, we could write a book on motivation that would both be scientifically sound and at the same time be highly practical. What you see is the result of that effort.

Finally, we want to acknowledge all the help we have received in putting this book together. Peter Ramstad helped greatly in thinking through the ideas in the early stage of the book's development. Bob's wife, Sandy, and his doctoral students read and commented on many different drafts, especially José David, Joel Philo, Dave McMonagle, Tori Youngcourt, Melissa Harrell, Dawn Safranek-Leonard, and Carol Thornston. Natalie Wright put the index together. Finally, students in Bob's Executive MBA classes shared excellent feedback that we incorporated throughout the text.

We hope that the concepts presented will be useful to you both professionally and personally.

Bob Pritchard
Elissa Ashwood

UNDERSTANDING MOTIVATION

Chapter 1

Motivation and Management

It's Monday morning. You step into your car and put the keys in the ignition. Unlike other mornings, the car doesn't spring to life. The dashboard's cheerful light blinks, "service engine soon." A few half-hearted sputters and several tries later, you are no further along. Is it the battery? The starter? Spark plugs? A computer chip? You don't know. It's so frustrating. You wonder how late you will be for work and how much this repair will cost you.

It's Monday afternoon. You are the manager of a customer service call center team. You walk past a group of telephone representatives on your way into a meeting with several other managers. You notice that most of them aren't smiling. In the meeting, you discuss lackluster customer satisfaction scores, high staff turnover rates, and concerns over upcoming performance appraisals. There is a palpable level of burnout in the air. You want to do something about it. But what? Add more staff? Get a better IT system? Hold a competition or a family picnic? You don't know. It's so frustrating. Your boss reminds you that motivation is your job as a manager.

Like the indicator light on a car dashboard, citing *motivation* as the catch-all reason for people's actions isn't specific enough to be useful. If the car won't start and the "service engine soon" light flickers on, you haven't learned anything about why the car won't start. You know that there are several possible reasons, some of them minor, some serious, but you won't be able to fix the car without a more detailed diagnosis than an indicator light can provide.

As a manager, what are you managing exactly? Management is about managing *behavior*. Management practices and systems are designed to *change* some aspect of behavior in order to improve effectiveness. To change behavior, you must understand motivation, the process that determines how people behave. Trying to manage without understanding motivation becomes an endless game of "whack-a-mole," an arcade game designed to see how many rodents you can hit with a bat as they pop out of numerous burrows. You tackle one problem, only to see another pop up elsewhere in a seemingly endless and random pattern.

This book is designed to help you better understand motivation in a more technical way so that you can successfully diagnose the specific reasons that the "indicator light" has turned on in yourself or in your group and to give you a clearer idea of where to begin to fix the problem. The following chapters will present the important components of motivation and how they work together based on leading research evidence. This more complex and detailed model of motivation will give you analytical tools to really understand and improve motivation.

Basic Assumptions About People

To put a motivation model in context, think about some basic assumptions about people.

People Have a Fundamental Need to Do a Good Job

You probably know people who don't care if they do a good job—people who don't seem to get any satisfaction out of doing a good job or dissatisfaction out of doing a bad job. So it may seem like doing a good job is a personal value, not a basic need. But have you ever seen a one-year-old loafing at a task? Children devote their complete attention and all of their effort to whatever they're doing. The inherent desire to do things well is an adaptive trait: it aids survival. Early humans who didn't do a job well weren't just downsized, they were eaten.

Not only do people want to do good work, they *feel good* when they do good work and *feel bad* when they do poor work. It is intrinsically satisfying to do things well and intrinsically dissatisfying to do things poorly. Again, think of small children trying to accomplish something. If they try repeatedly without success, they're frustrated and unhappy. When they succeed, they're delighted.

Over time, motivation fluctuates as we encounter situations that undermine our intrinsic desire to do a good job. Some of the things that decrease *work* motivation are objectives that keep changing, arbitrary performance standards, too few resources to get the work done, feedback that consists only of criticism, and disrespectful treatment. All of these things drive out motivation to do good work. The good news is that things can be changed that will increase the innate desire to do a good job. That is what this book is about.

People Want Control at Work

People want to feel that they have some influence on what happens to them in all aspects of their lives, including their work. This is also a very basic need. Think again of small children who become frustrated and angry when they can't reach something or can't communicate their wants. This need does not go away as we grow up; we just express our frustration in a different way. People also want control at work, and attempts made to understand and manage work motivation need to understand this. Many workplaces have experimented with expanding individual control as a strategy for increasing quality and innovation. In recent years, this idea has been called empowerment.

People Do Not Want to Be Held Accountable for Things They Cannot Control

It is common for people to be measured and evaluated on things they believe they cannot control. If I'm working on a project that depends on information from several other people, I resent being criticized for being late if the others didn't get me the information on time. While some aspects of work will always be outside a person's control, measurement and feedback systems that depend primarily on uncontrollable factors decrease predictability and, therefore, one's sense of control.

People Want Feedback but Don't Like to Be Evaluated

We all want to know how well we're doing—uncertainty is stressful—but no one likes to be *evaluated*. Evaluation is often an unpleasant experience, and unless the rating is highly favorable, it usually leads to negative reactions. What people really want is detailed feedback that no one else sees unless it is highly favorable—in which case, they want it published in the newspaper!

People Want to Be Valued

Have you ever found yourself feeling less motivated at work because you weren't feeling valued, only to have someone demonstrate their respect and appreciation for you and suddenly you're volunteering for extra assignments? Respect and appreciation are powerful.

People Do Not Want Their Time Wasted

Everyone's time is valuable. Showing respect for a person's time values that person. Wasting someone's time by communicating unclear priorities or by making constant changes to procedures decreases motivation. When you improve the motivation level in a work group, everyone's time is used more efficiently to produce a result.

So What Is Motivation?

The word *motivation* is sometimes used to describe how hard someone is willing to work to accomplish something: you might say that a colleague is highly motivated to finish project. It can also describe what inspires someone: one person may be motivated by recognition, another by pay raises. Motivation to diet or exercise conjures up images of the discipline required to do something unpleasant. And in offices everywhere, we watch for visible levels of enthusiasm, order pizza to compensate for low morale, and then describe this as motivation as well. Let's look at a more technical definition.

People have needs they want to satisfy. We behave in ways that we expect will satisfy those needs. *Needs* are like the magnet shown in Figure 1.1 that create an internal force to satisfy them. Think about being hungry: the hungrier you get, the stronger your desire to eat.

In a very simple model (see Figure 1.1), we can say that we use energy from our own personal *Energy Pool* to satisfy our *Needs. Motivation* is how we choose to allocate that energy to different actions to achieve the greatest satisfaction of our needs.

Motivation is the process used to allocate energy
to maximize the satisfaction of needs.

We allocate time and energy to different actions by deciding direction, effort, and persistence:

- *Direction:* Which actions we will work on
- *Effort:* How hard we will work on those actions
- *Persistence:* How long we will work on those actions

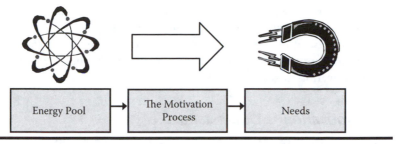

| Energy Pool | The Motivation Process | Needs |

Figure 1.1.

Problems can show up in any of these areas: you may be doing the wrong actions (direction), putting too little energy into an action (effort), or failing to work on an action long enough (persistence).

Suppose that each of three project managers does a poor job on a report. Assume that all three have the capability and the resources to do a good job.

The first one spends too much time on formatting the report and too little time on getting the content correct. This manager put too much effort into the wrong tasks, an error in *direction*. The second manager spent only a few hours on the report; not enough time to do a good job. The report required more *effort*. The third manager did not do the extra steps needed to get all the supplementary information needed to add to the report, so this manager didn't end up with a good report. Here the problem was *persistence*.

All these actions are made possible by the energy a person has available to allocate to actions. A motivating environment will be one where expending more energy leads to satisfying more needs.

Why Is Understanding Motivation So Important?

In the very simple model above, *motivation* represents how we allocate our energy to satisfy our needs. While there are many things that determine what our motivation will be, motivation influences everything we do!

People cannot always control the circumstances under which they work—the availability of information, the quality of equipment, the effectiveness of colleagues—nor the consequences of their actions. They can, however, control what they do. To increase performance and thereby improve the effectiveness of your organization, you want people to change how they do things. This means changing their behavior (and yours as well!). For people to change their behavior, they must change how they allocate energy to actions, i.e., they must change their motivation. Changing the right components of motivation in the right way leads to improved performance. In other words, you can't change behavior, and ultimately performance, without changing motivation.

We will use a more detailed model in the following chapters to more fully understand motivation. Before we get into that topic, here are nine features about motivation to keep in mind.

1. Motivation Is Understandable

The components of motivation make sense, yet this book will challenge you to think about many concepts at the same time. By understanding how these components work together, you can see your group's motivation as a logical process that you can diagnose and influence.

2. Motivation Is a Process

Motivation is a *process* in the sense that manufacturing is a process: a series of interconnected steps produces the end product. If one step goes awry, the whole process breaks down.

3. Motivation Is a Fundamental Issue, Not a Fad

The history of management includes many fads that have become popular and then died out. Focus on motivation is not a fad; motivation is basic. Understanding motivational principles can help you understand behavior and identify in advance what is going to work, no matter what changes in the work environment.

4. Motivation Is a Long-Term Issue

So called "motivational speakers" may get people excited about work, but the high is temporary. Managing motivation is less emotional and more long-lasting. A sustained effort to continually monitor, diagnose, and make improvements is needed.

5. Motivation Is Logical

Motivation operates on logical, understandable principles. With a good model of motivation, you can diagnose a situation and know what to do to improve it. Think about quality: there was a time when quality was seen as vague and difficult to manage, but now it can be defined, measured, and improved. You can understand and encourage motivation, just as you can understand and encourage quality.

6. *Motivation Is Manageable*

Because motivation is understandable, you can manage it. You can affect the amount of time and energy people spend on different tasks to increase their effectiveness.

Think about a person whose motivation seems to be low, who exerts minimal effort with little apparent interest in how much gets done or how well it is done. On weekends, that same person spends hours diligently working as a volunteer in the community. This is the same person; the difference is the work environment. It's not that you're lucky to have motivated people working for you or unlucky to have unmotivated people. How you manage has a significant influence on motivation.

7. *Motivation Is Also Work Strategy*

Motivation is more than the overall effort that goes into a job; it is also work strategy. Work strategy is choosing what to work on, what not to work on, how much effort to put into each possible task, and how to sequence this effort over time. It is also a central part of motivation.

8. *Motivation Is a Collaboration*

Motivation is a collaboration between the organization and its employees: staff members are asked to devote time and energy to the organization in exchange for pay and benefits. Thus, motivation is something the organization does *with* people not *to* people. Managing motivation is not manipulating people—in fact, it's just the opposite. Managing motivation means learning how to optimize staff contributions to the organization while at the same time improving how staff needs are satisfied. With knowledge and skill, you can work with the people you supervise to create a work environment that is highly motivating to them.

9. *With High Motivation, Everybody Wins*

Maximizing motivation benefits people as well as the organization. Think of jobs where you haven't felt strongly motivated. That kind of work is unpleasant, frustrating, boring, stressful, and fatiguing. In contrast, jobs that are highly motivating are more stimulating and more fun. When people can convert energy into satisfied needs efficiently, their energy actually increases. When they can't, energy decreases.

Using This Book

Improving motivation is a fascinating challenge that you can apply to yourself, to others, or to organizations. As an individual, you can use motivation analysis to improve your own life satisfaction or to enhance your career opportunities by developing your self-management skills. As a manager, understanding motivation can be particularly helpful when you are learning how to manage a group for the first time, entering an existing group as its new manager, or managing a group whose performance needs to improve. If you have responsibilities for leadership development in your organization, assessing and building motivation skills in the next generation of leaders can be done in a more formal and explainable way using the elements of motivation analysis. If you are starting up a new company or group you can use an understanding of motivation to set things up right from the start. Finally, motivation analysis can give you a roadmap for consulting with a group to improve effectiveness.

Motivational analysis can be used for any form of organization. In for-profit and not-for-profit organizations, hierarchical and flat organizations, formal and informal work groups, and across cultures, people are fundamentally affected by similar motivation principles.

One-Minute Assessment

Do you have a motivation problem? Start by taking the short quiz in Table 1.1. You can answer the questions for yourself or for your work group.

Symptoms of Low Motivation

Some of the signs of low motivation are obvious, some not so obvious. However, if the symptoms above are common in your work unit, you probably have a motivation problem.

Scoring:

21–30	**Green Light.** Motivation looks good.
31–45	**Yellow Light.** Some motivation problems.
46–63	**Red Light.** Serious motivation problems.

If your score is yellow or red, this book can help you improve things. If it is green, this book can help you keep it there.

Table 1.1. Motivation Symptoms Questionnaire: Do You Have a Motivation Problem?

Rarely or never	*Sometimes*	*Often*	*Do you or the people in your group ...*
1	2	3	Avoid unpleasant tasks
1	2	3	Work inefficiently and do not want to become more efficient
1	2	3	Focus on following rules rather than the best way to get the work done
1	2	3	Resist new ideas and new ways of doing things
1	2	3	Generate few innovative ideas
1	2	3	Put in the least possible amount of effort
1	2	3	Avoid taking on additional work
1	2	3	Avoid work—arriving late, leaving early, prolonged breaks or lunches, excessive Internet surfing, absenteeism
1	2	3	Not put in the effort to finish work properly
1	2	3	Give up on difficult tasks
1	2	3	Lack enthusiasm for the work
1	2	3	Have low job satisfaction
1	2	3	Have little loyalty to the unit or organization
1	2	3	Have low commitment to the goals of the unit or organization
1	2	3	Frequently report stress
1	2	3	Frequently report fatigue
1	2	3	Have chronic physical problems (fatigue, migraines, lower back pain, trouble sleeping)
1	2	3	Show a lack of cooperation with co-workers
1	2	3	Have frequent complaints about management and co-workers
1	2	3	Blame others for problems
1	2	3	Frequently complain about seemingly small issues
			Total score =

Key Points

- Management is about managing behavior.
- Management practices and systems are designed to change some aspect of behavior in order to improve effectiveness.
- Behavior is the only thing people can directly control.
- To change behavior, you must change motivation.
- Motivation is the process of allocating energy to actions that are expected to maximize need satisfaction.
- Learning the components of motivation and how they work together will help you diagnose problems and make improvements.
- Needs are the magnet that drives motivation.
- Energy is the time and effort available to meet those needs.
- Motivation includes direction, effort, and persistence.
- Motivation is a logical, understandable process that can be managed.
- Improving motivation in organizations is a win–win collaboration. The company benefits from better performance. Individuals benefit from better need satisfaction and increased energy to use in meeting more needs.

Chapter 2

Understanding Needs and Energy

Motivation is the process of turning energy into satisfied needs. Needs are represented in the simple motivation model shown in Figure 2.1 as a magnet because they have a powerful pull that compels us to action. The more powerful the need, the more energy we are willing to use to satisfy it.

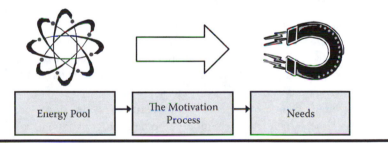

Figure 2.1.

The Energy Pool

The energy pool is the amount of physical, mental, and emotional resources a person has available to apply to different actions or tasks. The more energy available, the more tasks the person can do (*direction*), the higher the intensity level (*effort*) that can be used to do them, and the longer they can be done (*persistence*).

Having a high level of energy does not ensure that this energy will be applied to work, of course. It only means that it is available. However, if the energy pool is low, it sets an upper limit on the amount of energy that can be applied either to work or to any other setting. The amount of available energy expands and contracts over time depending on factors such as physical and emotional health, stress from within the job or outside the job, exercise, and sleep patterns.

The level of energy can also be influenced by how motivating our work is. Jobs low in motivation sap energy; jobs high in motivation can increase energy. Think about jobs you have had where you were highly motivated and where you were not so highly motivated. You probably had more overall energy on the highly motivating jobs.

Another payoff for increasing motivation
is adding to the energy available for work.

Needs

Research has yielded a number of models to describe human needs. Some name just a few very general needs while others contain dozens. Table 2.1 gives some examples. As the table suggests, there is no universal master list of needs.

How Strong Is a Need?

Although humans have largely the same basic needs, we differ in the strength of these needs. One person's need for security may be much stronger than another's; another person's need for social contact may be stronger than his or her need for power. Again, these differences are not in which needs we have, but rather in how strong the needs are.

The strength of our needs is relatively permanent and only changes very slowly over time. When management development programs use needs inventories or values assessment questionnaires, the results give some idea of the strength of certain needs. These tools are used to understand differences among group members and differences in ourselves from prior results. Comparing scores every few years can give some indication of changes in needs strength.

While these instruments give us a picture of some of our needs, we usually have an inaccurate picture of the strength of all our needs. Part of this difficulty is that needs can be unconscious or subconscious, so we may not be particularly aware of some of them. For example, people with a high need for control may describe themselves as sharing power and being highly democratic even as they make all decisions without incorporating input from others. Another person's actions can-

Table 2.1. Theories of Needs

Alderfer

Existence: Basic human survival including physiological and safety needs
Relatedness: Having positive relationships with others
Growth: To have positive self development

Maslow

Physiological: Having adequate air, food, water, and sex
Security: Having adequate housing, clothing, and freedom from worry and
  anxiety
Self-belongingness/social: Having friends and feeling like you fit into a social
  network
Esteem: Being thought well of by others and feeling positive about the self
Self-actualization: Developing one's full potential

Dawis and Loftquist: Personnel Decisions, International

Achievement: To personally accomplish difficult tasks
Autonomy: To act independently and express creativity
Status: To get recognition, prestige, and authority
Relationships: To build strong relationships and be of service to others
Safety: To have security and stability
Comfort: To have a safe, comfortable, and low stress environment

Murray

Achievement: Accomplishing difficult tasks
Affiliation: Being with friends, having social contacts
Aggression: Being in situations of combat and argument
Autonomy: Freedom to act as one wishes, breaking away from restraints
Exhibition: Being the center of attention, enjoying having an audience
Impulsivity: Acting quickly and without much thought, easily venting
  feelings and ideas
Nurturance: Assisting others when possible, being sympathetic and
  comforting
Order: Keeping one's environment (self, others, physical environment) neat
  and organized
Power: Having control over people and one's environment
Understanding: Mastering areas of knowledge, satisfying intellectual
  curiosity

not always tell you about that person's needs. A leader who spends the day speaking with groups of people may still have a significant need for time alone.

> *It is difficult to get a clear picture of the strength of our own needs and even more difficult to know the strength of someone else's needs.*

A mistake we make is to assume that we know someone else's needs. Sometimes we make the error of assuming that their needs are similar to ours. This is especially true if they are similar to us in age, gender, race, and economic status. Or, when people are very different from us, we may make the opposite error and assume that their needs are completely different from ours. The point here is that it is difficult to assess accurately the strength of our own needs and even more difficult to assess the strength of others' needs.

Need Satisfaction and Dissatisfaction

The more fully our needs are met, the more need satisfaction we feel. The more our needs are not met, the more need dissatisfaction we feel. When we are very hungry, we feel uncomfortable. The hungrier we are, the more uncomfortable we feel. Need satisfaction feels good, we like it, and we try to achieve it. Conversely, need dissatisfaction feels bad, we do not like it, and we try to avoid it.

Need Strength Versus Need Satisfaction

Need satisfaction is different from needs and the strength of needs. Needs and the strength of one's needs are relatively permanent. In contrast, need satisfaction fluctuates fairly rapidly. Need satisfaction is a temporary state that is a function of what has happened to a person fairly recently. You eat a meal and your need for food is satisfied. As hours pass, this need satisfaction decreases and you experience need dissatisfaction in the form of hunger. That hunger motivates you to eat again. The *strength of your need* for food has not changed, but the *satisfaction of your need* for food has changed. At work, your need for achievement may be satisfied by a promotion and this satisfaction may last for some time. Eventually, however, the level of satisfaction of your need for achievement will decrease and you will want another promotion or something else that satisfies your achievement need.

Actual Versus Anticipated Need Satisfaction

The final point about needs is the difference between actual need satisfaction and anticipated need satisfaction. Actual need satisfaction is the satisfaction we feel after we get the desired outcome. It is how satisfied we are when we eat the meal, get the raise, or go to the party. It happens *after* we get the outcome. Anticipated need satisfaction is how much need satisfaction we *expect* to feel if we get the food, get the raise, or go to the party. It is present *before* we get the outcome. We can think of anticipated need satisfaction as desire. It is how much we want or desire the outcome.

Desire and actual need satisfaction are frequently not the same. We have all had the experience of a strong desire for something we thought would make us happy. More precisely, we expected it to produce strong need satisfaction. But the new car, the promotion, or the new relationship did not actually produce the need satisfaction we thought it would. On the other hand, actual need satisfaction may also be better than anticipated need satisfaction. Getting what we wanted can be even more satisfying than we thought it would be.

This idea of anticipated satisfaction is important because what we think will happen *in the future* guides our motivation. What is important is what we *expect* will happen. In contrast, job satisfaction is determined by how well our needs have actually been satisfied on the job *in the past*. Motivation is about doing things that will maximize our need satisfaction *in the future*.

> *Motivation is guided by how satisfying we think something is going to be. However, what we anticipate may not match the reality.*

This is what is known as an expectancy approach to motivation. Expectancy models of motivation have been around since the early 1900s and have been applied to work motivation since the mid-1960s. For example, Vroom's classic volume *Work and Motivation* (1964) was an expectancy model. Other expectancy models have been developed since then such as those by Graen (1969), Campbell and Pritchard (1976); Heckhousen (1991); Kanfer (1990, 1992); Mitchell and Daniels (2003). The motivation model used in this book comes most directly from the motivation model in Naylor, Pritchard, and Ilgen (1980).

Using What We Know About Needs

So how can we use this information about needs? Understanding needs leads to a very important point about motivation. Suppose a manager creates an incentive program where the participants are promised a scuba diving trip to the Great Barrier Reef in Australia? Let's look at the motivation such a reward might generate in each of three different people.

David does not enjoy being out on the beach and long airplane flights over the ocean cause him considerable anxiety. Clearly, the "reward" of the scuba trip will not meet David's needs. David will not be motivated to achieve the incentive. In fact, it would be a demotivator. This is in stark contrast to Nancy. Nancy loves the ocean and has always wanted to scuba dive, but lives far from the coast. There is little doubt in Nancy's mind that the trip would produce a very high level of need satisfaction. The incentive will be a powerful one for Nancy. Finally, there is Bill. Bill loves to scuba dive and lives in Hawaii where he dives many weekends. While diving is very attractive for Bill, little motivation would be created by this trip, as his needs are already being met.

People will not be motivated by rewards
that don't satisfy their needs.

Key Points

- Needs are the ultimate source of motivation.
- The Energy Pool is the amount of physical, mental, and emotional resources available to apply to actions or tasks. The more energy available, the more tasks the person can do (direction), the higher the intensity level (effort) that can be used to do them, and the longer they can be done (persistence).
- Energy is used to satisfy needs.
- We all have essentially the same needs, but we differ in the strength of these needs.
- It is difficult to get a clear picture of the strength of our own needs, and even more difficult to get a picture of the strength of someone else's needs.
- The more our needs are met, the more need satisfaction occurs. The less our needs are met, the more need dissatisfaction occurs.
- While the strength of needs is quite stable, the level of need satisfaction is temporary. It changes frequently depending on how well our needs are being met.
- What motivates us is the expectation of how satisfying something will be in the future. What we anticipate may not match the reality.
- People cannot be motivated with rewards that do not satisfy their needs.

Chapter 3

Understanding Motivation

People who have the energy available to satisfy their needs often don't apply that energy in a way that is optimal for the organization. Why? Somewhere in the motivation chain, the process is broken. If you want to fix the problem, but have very little understanding of how the process works, it is difficult to diagnose what's wrong. If all you can do with a car that won't start is check the gas gauge, you won't get far. If your understanding is more complete, you will have many more possibilities to check out, you will know what you are looking for, and you can tell where there is a problem. This understanding means that you will have a greater chance to *fix* the car.

To fix a car, a mechanic needs to understand how the components of the car work together. To change behavior, you need to understand the components of motivation and how they work together.

The Five Components of Motivation

The motivation process can be broken down into the five connected components shown in Figure 3.1: Actions, results, evaluations, outcomes, and need satisfaction.

Actions

An action is something you do—putting energy into a particular act or task. To help explain these components, consider the example of Ann, a marketing manager

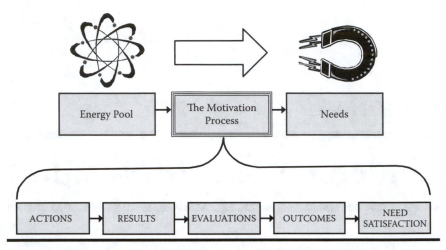

Figure 3.1. The expanded motivation model.

responsible for a new product launch. Some of Ann's actions may be observable by others, such as participating in a staff meeting or leading a focus group with potential customers. Other actions, such as considering alternative distribution channels, are not observable. These actions are known only to Ann.

Ann chooses the actions to which she will apply energy (direction), how much energy she will apply to each action (effort), and how long to apply energy to that action (persistence). These decisions occur continuously and often with little conscious thought. For example, suppose Ann must update a project status report each month. She has done this many times previously and knows that she must summarize key events of the past month, update the launch schedule, format the information, print the report, and distribute it. Without really thinking about it, Ann allocates energy to the relevant actions (direction) with a certain level of energy (effort) until the update is complete (persistence).

Writing monthly status reports is just one of many tasks to which Ann must allocate energy. Other activities that are part of her job include supervising analysts, participating in marketing plans for other products, and coordinating with manufacturing.

Finally, Ann's energy allocation to actions goes beyond just the work tasks. She also has to balance how much energy to apply to work and how much to apply to activities outside of work.

Results

Applying energy to actions generates *results*. Ann's work on the status report produces a result: a finished report. Observing a focus group of potential customers produces a result: insights about what customers think of a new product. Analyzing alternative distribution channels produces a result: a recommended distribution channel. These examples illustrate the fact that results range from the tangible, such as the report, to the intangible, such as insights about future customers.

Results—tangible and intangible, observed or not observed—create value for the organization. This value can be positive, negative, or neutral. One tangible, observable result of Ann's work is the product launch. If it goes well, it creates positive value. If it goes badly, it creates negative value.

> ***Energy applied to actions produces results.***

Evaluations

Evaluations are assessments of the value that results create. Put another way, how valuable is the result? Evaluations are made of the creativity of Ann's marketing plan, whether she stays within her budget, and how effectively she develops subordinates. In another setting, an evaluation could assess how securely a weld holds, the cleanliness of a floor, or the clarity of a vision statement.

In order for Ann's results to be evaluated, they must be observed or measured in some way. Ann generates many results; some are noticed by others and some are not. Results are observed with varying degrees of attention ranging from casual observation to careful quantitative measurement. Ann's manager probably wouldn't pay much attention if Ann put more plants in her office. Her manager would pay more attention if members of the project team expressed increased optimism or frustration about their progress. The manager probably would carefully measure the time required to launch the product, the expenses incurred, and the eventual success or failure of the new product.

In general, the more important the result is to the organization, the more likely it is to be carefully observed and measured. However, it is also common that some important results are neither observed nor measured. For example, customer satisfaction is usually an important result which adds considerable value. However, it may not be measured because doing so accurately is difficult. It will be hard for the manager to motivate employees to make customer satisfaction a priority when it is not measured.

It is important to understand that *a measure determines how much* there is of a result. *An evaluation determines how good or bad* that amount of the result is. Measures can range from a specific quantitative number to a casual observation. Some form of measurement always occurs before an evaluation is made, but measuring and evaluating can be nearly simultaneous.

Measures tell us what was done.
Evaluations tell us whether that amount is good or bad.

When Ann submits her report, some aspects of the report are measured and evaluated, and some are not. Ann's manager sees that the report is formatted slightly differently from usual and that it contains a substantial error. He attaches no significance (no evaluation) to the formatting change, but *measures* the report as having an error. In the manager's mind, the measured result, the report with the error, is placed on an evaluative continuum ranging from good to neutral to bad and is *evaluated* as bad. In our example, there would probably be little time between the boss noticing the error and the negative evaluation.

As the example above indicates, *evaluations vary in formality.* An annual performance appraisal is a formal evaluation. The daily evaluations we make of our own or someone else's results are less formal. The term *evaluation* refers here to all kinds of evaluations, not just formal reviews.

Evaluations can range from formal to very informal.

We usually do not even know all the evaluations that are made of our results because *more than one person evaluates results.* Ann's manager evaluates her results, and Ann herself notes what she has done on the distribution strategy (she measures her result) and decides how good a job she did (she evaluates her results). Ann's peers and subordinates, and people outside the organization—clients, suppliers, family, friends—also observe and evaluate some of her results.

Evaluations made by people at work assess the contribution the result makes to the organization. But *an evaluation may or may not accurately reflect the true value of the results to the organization.* Ann's boss may evaluate her report favorably because of its colorful graphics and ignore fatal flaws in the plan it describes. A colleague could see Ann leaving the office early and make the evaluation that she was not working hard, when she was actually leaving the office to work with the brochure printing vendor, a task that would keep her working late into the evening.

Many evaluations are made of our results.
These evaluations may or may not be accurate.

It is also common for people in different parts of the organization to evaluate results differently. This is evident in annual compensation reviews when executives debate over why their group deserves a larger share of the bonus pool. An even bigger problem occurs if measures and evaluations of a work unit are not aligned with the objectives of the overall organization. In this case, the work group may achieve its local goals at the expense of the larger organization.

Outcomes

Outcomes are the good and bad things that happen as a result of the evaluations of our actions. At work, these could include promotions, recognition, pay actions, retirement benefits, feelings of achievement, criticism, and desirable or undesirable working conditions.

We experience outcomes on a continuum of positive—a big raise!—to negative, such as being fired or publicly criticized. Some outcomes are neutral. Some outcomes are tangible, such as a salary, a corner office, or not getting an award, while others are intangible such as frustration over a mistake, a reputation for integrity, increased autonomy on projects, or compliments by a peer.

We can also give *ourselves* outcomes: a feeling of accomplishment for good work or anxiety about not finishing a task on time. Outcomes come from everywhere. When Ann consistently works late, she gets outcomes—some positive, some negative—from her manager, her assistant, and her family.

Need Satisfaction

The last step in the process is need satisfaction. We discussed need satisfaction in the previous chapter, but now we will be more specific. Need satisfaction comes from the outcomes that are received. The more need satisfaction we expect from an outcome, the more attractive the outcome. Because the strength of people's needs differ, the amount of need satisfaction a given outcome produces varies for each of us. A large pay raise could be a positive outcome because it satisfies Ann's needs for security, accomplishment, and achievement. But if it means pressure from her spouse to move into a more expensive house that Ann doesn't want, it may be neutral or even negative.

> *People will only be motivated if they expect that their actions will lead to outcomes that satisfy their needs.*

Sometimes we anticipate need satisfaction accurately, but sometimes the actual need satisfaction is very different from what we expect. Ann may expect that a promotion will be positive, but if she finds that she has a much heavier workload and some of her former colleagues resent her, the outcome is not as positive as she had anticipated.

Remember that motivation is *future* oriented: it is the *expected* satisfaction that determines behavior. Ann anticipates the degree of positive or negative satisfaction she will experience from an outcome. If she expects positive need satisfaction from the outcome, she will apply energy to actions in a way that she believes will create the results that will be evaluated in a way that will get her the outcome.

Maximizing Motivation

When we put all the components together, we have a more specific statement of when motivation will be high:

> *Motivation is high when a person has sufficient energy and believes he or she can apply this energy to actions that will produce results that will be positively evaluated and lead to outcomes that satisfy needs.*

Key Points

- To change behavior, you need to understand the components of motivation and how they work together.
- The motivation process can be broken down into five connected components: actions, results, evaluations, outcomes, and need satisfaction.
- An action is something you do—putting energy into a particular act or task. Actions can be observable or unobservable.
- Results are created by the action. They can be tangible and intangible; observed or not observed.
- Evaluations are assessments of the value that results create for the person or the organization. In order for results to be evaluated, they must be observed or measured in some way. Measures tell us what was done. Evaluations tell us whether that amount is good or bad.
- Evaluations range from the formal to informal.
- Evaluations are made by ourselves and by multiple people inside and outside the organization. They may or may not accurately reflect the true value of the results to the organization.
- Outcomes are the good, neutral, and bad things that happen as a result of the evaluations of our actions.
- Outcomes lead to need satisfaction. The more need satisfaction we expect from an outcome, the more attractive the outcome. Actual need satisfaction can be quite different from expected need satisfaction.
- Motivation is high when a person has sufficient energy and believes he or she can apply this energy to actions that will produce results that will be positively evaluated and lead to outcomes that satisfy needs.

Chapter 4

Dynamics of the Motivation Model

The five components of the motivation process work together. We devote energy to actions, actions produce results, these results are evaluated, and the evaluations produce outcomes that may or may not lead to need satisfaction. The circled arrows in Figure 4.1 represent the connections between each component.

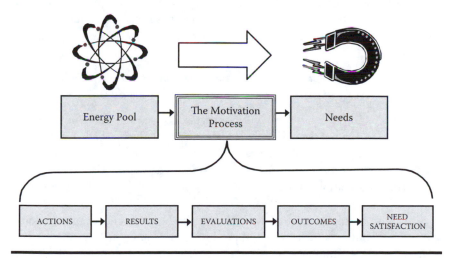

Figure 4.1.   Connections in the expanded motivation model.

This chapter emphasizes the importance of these connections between the components because it is the *strength of the connections* that determines how well the motivation process is working.

Action-to-Results Connections

The connection between actions and results is the degree to which a person's actions control the result that he or she produces. More precisely, it is the perceived *relationship* between the amount of energy devoted to the action and the quality of the result that will be produced. When Ann weeds her flowerbeds, there is a clear connection between the effort she puts into weeding (the action) and how much of the flowerbed is finished (the result). Additional effort leads to more of the flowerbed getting weeded. This is an example of a strong action-to-results connection.

Consider another task: repairing the transmission of a car. Ann has little knowledge of car repair. No matter how much energy she puts into fixing the transmission, it is not going to get fixed. This is an example of a weak action-to-results connection: there is *no relationship* between the energy expended and the result.

You may ask: If Ann doesn't know anything about fixing transmissions, why would she even *try* to fix it? That's the point of this example: if there is no relationship between the effort you put into a task and how much of it gets done, you have no motivation to do it. If we offered Ann $10,000 to fix the transmission with no outside help, she is still unlikely to try because the action-to-results connection is so weak. Ann would not be *motivated* to do the task, even with a large incentive.

> *When action-to-results connections are low,*
> *you have little control over the results produced.*

Consider another example that is more typical of tasks at work. Suppose that Ann has to do the quarterly budget for her product launch. She knows how to do the budget, but needs information on how much of each task on the plan has been completed and realistic estimates of time needed to finish the remaining tasks. This information comes from other people and it is often not completely accurate.

This is an example of a moderate relationship between effort put into doing the quarterly budget (the action) and producing the budget (the result). In general, if Ann puts in more effort, she will produce the budget more quickly and it will be a better budget—but she can also waste a lot of time searching for information that turns out to be unreliable. The relationship between effort and results for the budget is stronger than for the transmission, but weaker than for weeding her garden.

Don't expect people to be highly motivated
when they cannot control their results.

The relationship between actions and results can be pictured graphically for any action. Viewing these graphs side by side can help to illustrate the differences between a weak connection and a strong one.

In each of the three graphs in Figure 4.2, the horizontal axis represents the amount of energy devoted to the action; the vertical axis represents the amount of the result produced.

The first graph shows a strong positive relationship between amount of energy expended on weeding and the amount of the garden that gets weeded. The relationship is linear and steep for most levels of energy, but then Ann begins to get tired and reaches a point of diminishing returns—the leveling off of the slope at high levels of effort—where she becomes less efficient and gets less weeding finished for each additional unit of energy.

The transmission repair example in the middle graphic with the flat line shows no relationship between effort and results; no amount of energy can move the project forward.

In the budgeting example (the third graph), the overall relationship is positive, but not nearly as steep as for weeding. Because Ann has less control over budgeting than she has over weeding, expending more energy does not have nearly as much effect on the results. This is shown by the less steep slope for budgeting. In addition, the point of diminishing returns—where the function starts to flatten—occurs earlier than for weeding. This suggests that putting high levels of energy into the task will not get it finished much more quickly or more accurately.

The key here is what a person *believes* the strength of the action-to-results connections are. Suppose that the three graphs in Figure 4-2 represent tasks that are all part of Ann's job. If we didn't know anything else, these graphs say that she will devote a fairly high level of energy to the first task, none to the second task, and a moderate amount of energy to the third task. The perceived connections influence how Ann allocates energy to tasks—that is, they influence Ann's motivation.

Results-to-Evaluation Connections

A results-to-evaluation connection is the perceived relationship between the amount of the result that is produced and the favorableness of the evaluation by

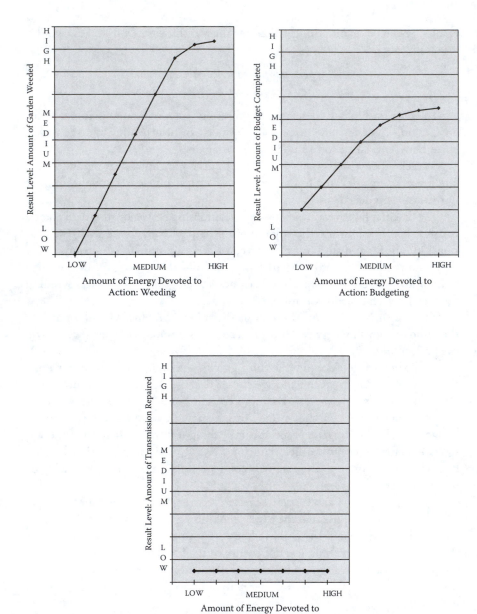

Figure 4.2.   Action-to-results connections.

a given evaluator. As with action-to-results connections, the issue is the expected relationship between the two.

In Figure 4.3, the horizontal axis is now the amount of the result that is produced, ranging from low to high. The vertical axis is favorableness of the evaluation, ranging from very negative through neutral to very positive.

The first graph shows a steep straight line between the speed of Ann's launch of the new product and how favorably she is evaluated by her manager: the faster the launch, the more positive the evaluation. In other words, the faster the launch, the more value that is created for the organization. Each unit of increase in the speed of the launch adds an equal amount of value to the organization.

The second graph represents how accurately Ann's quarterly budget matches actual expenditures. This relationship starts to reach a point of diminishing returns at the point where her accuracy passes the medium level. This indicates that as long as the budget is reasonably close to actual expenditures, the evaluation is positive; greater accuracy adds little value.

The overall slope of this result is less steep than for speed of product launch: budget accuracy is not as important to the organization as speed of product launch. Put another way, variations in budget accuracy have a smaller effect on the value to the organization than variations in the speed of product launch. The budget connection is an example of a result that has a large downside value and a much smaller upside value.

The third graph indicates that it is important for Ann to do some training of her staff, but there is no benefit for going from moderate to high levels of training. Ann's evaluation would not improve if she provided high rather than moderate amounts of training for her staff.

In this example, Ann should continually try to increase the speed of product launch, produce budgets that are moderately accurate but not put much effort into getting beyond moderate accuracy, and do some training but not too much.

As a manager accountable for deciding how to use limited resources, the concept of results-to-evaluation connections is very useful in determining how to prioritize. You put energy toward the things that are most valuable to the organization. A results-to-evaluation graph is essentially an economic utility curve describing how much value will be generated for a given level of the result.

These connections define the evaluation system because they specify how results are valued. This defines policy and determines priorities. What frequently happens is that priorities are not clear. Think of times you were perfectly happy to spend time and energy doing any of the tasks on your job but weren't clear on priorities. This is an uncomfortable situation, made even more uncomfortable when you are criticized by your boss (an outcome) because you spent too much time on one thing (an action) and not enough on another. In motivational

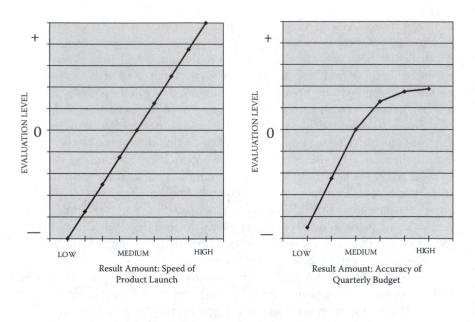

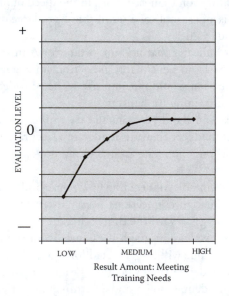

Figure 4.3.   Results-to-evaluation connections.

terms, you allocated too much energy to the wrong actions because you did not have clear results-to-evaluation connections. Lack of effort wasn't the problem; you simply didn't have the information you needed about priorities.

So one of the keys to high motivation is to make sure the results-to-evaluation connections are high and are clear. If they are inaccurate or unclear, people will not know how to maximally allocate their efforts. They do not know how to act in order to get positive evaluations. This decreases motivation.

> *A person must know how different results are valued for motivation to be high.*

To complicate matters, results-to-evaluation connections are different for different evaluators. Many people, both inside and outside the organization, evaluate Ann's results, and they disagree about the most important things to be done.

Knowing that this difference exists and trying to live with it produce conflict. Not knowing that differences in priorities exist is also surprisingly common. It has happened to all of us that we think we are doing a good job and others evaluate us less positively because we have not been prioritizing our efforts the way the evaluator prioritizes them. This can be a real shock and be very dissatisfying. If it goes on long enough, it can produce a decrease in effort or withdrawal from the organization. Serious motivation problems often develop as a result of lack of agreement on results-to-evaluations connections.

Evaluation-to-Outcome Connections

An evaluation-to-outcome connection is the perceived relationship between the favorableness of the evaluation and the expected amount of an outcome. Recall that outcomes are intrinsic and extrinsic rewards and punishments.

In Figure 4.4, the horizontal axis is the favorableness of the evaluation and the vertical axis is the amount of the outcome the person believes will follow. The top two graphs deal with the outcome of a pay raise. The one on the left is typical of many management pay systems: if the evaluation is negative to neutral, the person gets a modest raise—a cost-of-living raise. Even poor performers get a minimum raise. The raise is larger as the evaluation becomes more positive.

The graph on the right represents an across-the-board pay raise: everyone gets a moderate raise. Because everyone gets the same raise, there is no relationship between performance on the job (the evaluation) and the size of the raise. This produces a flat line in the graph.

The lower pair of graphs represent an internally generated outcome: a feeling of personal accomplishment. Assume that the source of Ann's evaluation is

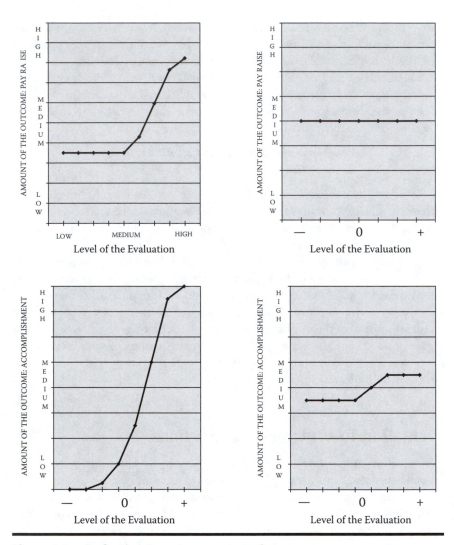

Figure 4.4. Evaluation-to-outcome connections.

her direct manager. The graph on the left indicates that her feelings of accomplishment are closely tied to her manager's evaluation. If that evaluation is low, Ann feels a low level of accomplishment. The steep increase shows that her feelings of accomplishment increase rapidly as her manager's evaluation gets more positive.

The graph on the right shows only a small relationship between the favorableness of the evaluation and Ann's feeling of accomplishment. This might indicate that Ann does not believe that her manager is a good judge of her work, so her sense of accomplishment doesn't change much based on his evaluation. A positive evaluation is a little better than a negative evaluation, but not much better.

Evaluation-to-outcome connections are usually different for different evaluators. The evaluations of Ann's work by her boss, her peers, her subordinates, and herself frequently result in different outcomes or different levels of the same outcome.

Different evaluators *control* different outcomes. Evaluations by Ann's boss influence outcomes such as raises and work assignments. Ann's acceptance by her peers is an outcome given by co-workers, not the boss. Outcomes such as a personal feeling of accomplishment are controlled by Ann herself.

As with the other connections, maximizing motivation requires that the evaluation-to-outcome connections be high. If they are not, people see little or no tie between their performance and the outcomes they receive. So even if Ann can control the effort to produce results that are valued, there is no incentive for her to do so if her good performance does not lead to substantially more positive outcomes than her poor performance would.

> ***Outcomes that are not tied to performance will have little
> or no effect on the motivation to do a better job.***

Outcome-to-Need Satisfaction Connections

The outcome-to-need satisfaction connection is the perceived relationship between the level of an outcome and the level of anticipated need satisfaction. How much does a person want of a specified amount of the outcome? These connections are unique to each person depending on how that person values different outcomes.

In Figure 4.5, the horizontal axis is the level of the outcome, and the vertical axis is the anticipated need satisfaction. Negative anticipated need satisfaction means that you believe that the outcome will produce *dissatisfaction*. If anticipated need satisfaction is neutral, the zero point on the graph, the outcome is not expected to produce either satisfaction or dissatisfaction.

The outcome in the top two graphs is income. Suppose the graph on the left is Ann's outcome-to-need satisfaction. The steep curve indicates that Ann has a high desire for money; low levels of it are very dissatisfying and high levels are satisfying. Only when income is very high does the gain in anticipated value start to taper off. In contrast, suppose the graph on the right is for Ann's co-worker Dave. This curve levels off near moderate levels of income. For Dave, having a moderate level of income is important—the connection graphic is steep up to medium income levels—but once he has a medium level of income, he sees little value in making more money.

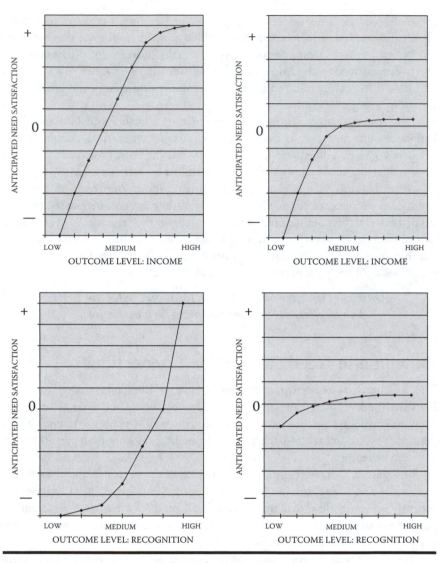

Figure 4.5. Outcome-to-need satisfaction connections.

If both Ann and Dave have moderate salaries and we offer more money for higher performance, Ann's performance might increase, but not Dave's. Ann would anticipate that an increase in the amount of the outcome would increase her need satisfaction, whereas Dave would anticipate that an increase would not lead to increased need satisfaction.

The outcome in the bottom two graphs is less tangible: recognition. The function on the left starts out slowly and then increases very rapidly. Let's assume this is Ann. She values a lot of recognition. Low or even moderate levels of recognition are not nearly enough to produce need satisfaction for her. In fact, even moderately high levels of recognition are aversive: they produce dissatisfaction in that they do not lead to satisfaction levels above zero. It takes a lot of recognition to produce any need satisfaction, and when recognition is high, she anticipates a high level of need satisfaction. Ann is happy only when she gets very high amounts of recognition.

The connection for Dave, shown in the graph on the right, is very different. The relative flatness indicates that different levels of recognition do not have much effect on Dave's need satisfaction. Low levels of recognition are slightly— but only slightly—negative. Even high levels of recognition are only slightly positive. Using recognition to motivate Ann could be very effective, but it would have almost no effect on Dave.

> *One of the challenges of managing motivation is learning*
> *what outcomes are effective for different people.*

Rewards (outcomes) are important motivational tools but, as we have seen, the connections tell us that the same reward does not have the same effect on everyone. To use rewards effectively, a manager needs to know how important a given outcome is to different individuals.

So why not just ask? How important is money, promotions, or feelings of achievement? This is really the wrong question. The important issue is the *relationship* between level of the outcome (money, for example) and anticipated need satisfaction. One practical approach is to ask how valuable would an *increase* in the outcome be? This is a better way to assess the connection than asking how important the outcome is.

It may be very important to Dave to make enough money to meet his family's basic needs and to have a bit left over, but after that, more is not important to him. If he is not making enough for necessities, then making more is *very* valuable. This issue is important in using the model for diagnosing motivation, as we will see in later chapters.

Awareness of Components of the Model

Clearly, no one goes around consciously thinking about results-to-evaluation connections or which outcomes are tied to which needs. If we had to consciously go through all of the motivational components for every action, we wouldn't get much done.

In our conscious thoughts we focus on the results component. Ann thinks about a meeting to discuss details of the ad campaign for the new product launch, the decision she needs to make about whether to keep using the same supplier of marketing data, and how she is going to staff a new project. Each of these is a result. Then she plans her day—that is, she decides how to allocate effort to actions to achieve these results.

While Ann focuses on results and is rarely thinking of the other components of the model, they are influencing her. At some level, she has considered them and made decisions about how to spend her time and effort based on her perceptions of the components.

We usually don't think about most components of the model, but they still influence us.

We know that the model components are influencing us because they are *retrievable*. If someone asks Ann the right questions, she can describe the other motivation components. Suppose Ann has decided to finalize the staffing of the new project. If we asked her to describe how she will go about getting the necessary information to make that decision, she could tell us—she could describe how she will allocate energy to specific actions to produce the result of the staffing decisions. She is describing the action-to-results connections she believes exist to produce that result. If we asked her who would evaluate her staffing decisions, she could tell us. She could also give us some idea of the results-to-evaluation connections by describing what measures or criteria evaluators would use to make their evaluations. If we asked her what outcomes those evaluators would give her based on their evaluations, she might say she sees few outcomes that would come from her boss or peers. This is a perception of the evaluation-to-outcome connections: she is saying they are very low. She could also tell us how important different outcomes are to her. In doing so, she would be describing her own outcome-to-need satisfaction connections.

The fact that the motivation components are retrievable makes it possible to diagnose them and to make improvements based on the diagnoses.

Sometimes, especially when something unexpected happens, you *do* think about all the components of the model. You work hard on a project but can't seem to get it finished. You thought you had a good strategy, but it is unexpectedly not working—the way you are allocating energy to different possible actions is not producing the results. Your action-to-results connections need to be changed. When the evaluation you get from your manager is significantly different from what you had expected, you think about what results the manager is focusing on to make that evaluation. You are thinking about results-to-evaluation connections. If you do not get the promotion or the raise you expected, you realize that your ideas about how to get these outcomes are not correct. You start thinking about evaluation-to-outcome connections. Finally, if you get the outcome of the new job assignment and it does not produce the satisfaction you expected, you start to explore outcome-to-need satisfaction connections.

> ***We think about the motivation components***
> ***when something unexpected happens.***

How are these connections formed in the first place? One source is *experience*. For example, we devote effort to an action and we see what the results are. Over time, we form an expectation of the connection between an action and the result. This expectation may or may not be accurate, but it is what we believe is true.

Another way of forming connections is *information*: we can be *told* what the connection is. For example, a manager or co-worker can suggest a better way to do something.

Finally, we can *observe* how someone else allocates effort to actions and we see the results. This can lead us to change our perceived connections and thus how we allocate energy to those tasks.

Motivation as a Process

A major point with which to end this chapter is one of the most critical points in this entire book. It is that motivation has a number of components and for motivation to be high, *all* these components must be favorable. If just one is low, motivation will be low. We have said motivation is a process. With all processes, there is a series of steps that must happen. It is typical that if even one of the steps in the process is not going well, the whole process suffers. This is true whether one is baking a cake, refining petroleum, or developing new drugs for a pharmaceutical company. If everything in the process is done well, output is high. However, if just *one step* is not done well, output will suffer. For example, if every step in the motivation process is fine except that the evaluations of results are seen as capricious or invalid, that one problem can substantially reduce motivation.

If all the components are in good condition, motivation is high. If they are not, motivation is not so high.

> ***For motivation to be high,***
> ***all the components of the model must be high.***

We said at the start of the book that to manage motivation we must first understand the motivation model. This chapter concludes our presentation of that model. The next steps in being able to manage motivation are diagnosing and then making improvements. We now move to the diagnosis section of the book.

Key Points

- The five components of the motivation process work together. The strength of the connections determines whether or not motivation is high.
- Action-to-results connections describe the relationship between how much energy is put into the action and how much of the result is produced.
- Don't expect people to be motivated when they have little control over their results.
- Results-to-evaluation connections describe the relationship between the amount of the result produced and the favorableness of the evaluation.
- A person must know how different results are valued in order for motivation to be high.
- Results-to-evaluation connections reflect what an evaluator thinks is important. Ideally, they reflect how results add value to the organization. Awareness of results-to-evaluation connections is essential for understanding priorities.
- Evaluation-to-outcome connections describe the relationship between the favorableness of the evaluation and the amount of the outcome expected.
- Evaluation-to-outcome connections are different for different evaluators. Different evaluators control different outcomes.
- Outcomes that are not tied to performance won't improve performance.
- Outcome-to-need satisfaction connections describe the relationship between the amount of the outcome and the anticipated level of satisfaction or dissatisfaction.
- The strength of these connections is unique to each person and reflects how one values different outcomes. Knowing how much someone values a specific amount of an outcome is very useful for creating a motivating reward system.
- Although we are not consciously aware of most of the motivation components, they still influence us.
- We simplify by focusing on results, but we can retrieve our perceptions of the other components of the model if we are asked the right questions. This allows us to diagnose the motivation process.
- We focus on the connections when something unexpected happens.
- Connections are formed based on experience, information, and observation.
- For motivation to be high, all components and their connections must be strong. If just one is weak, motivation will be low.

DIAGNOSING AND IMPROVING MOTIVATION

This section starts a case study that we will use throughout the rest of the book. The purpose of the case is to illustrate some of the motivation issues described in the book in the context of a realistic business setting. A single case cannot cover all the issues raised in the book but a number of issues will be illustrated. Although there is no single correct approach to a complex business issue, insights from this case may apply to your own situation. In addition to the course of action presented here, consider how you would apply the motivation model yourself if you were in the manager's role, or a consultant to the manager.

An Extended Case Study

Friday, March 1, 3 p.m. Conference Call

"Thank you, and have a great weekend!" Jessica Thorpe cheerily closed out her weekly regional sales conference call. Sighing, she looked at the month's sales numbers again. Of the four territories

she supervised, only Midwest was beating its target. Although Midwest's numbers were impressive, they couldn't carry the rest of the country. She knew the group would have to do better. They were heading into the second quarter and if they didn't catch up soon, they wouldn't have a chance at making the full year's goal.

Jessica thought about all she had done to help drive performance. She had provided plenty of encouragement and regular contact. Resources were always tight, but she felt her team got what they really needed. Turnover wasn't too high. The market was pretty good; she'd seen worse. Of the four regional managers, Jose, Dave, Susan, and Marius, only Marius was really new to the role and he seemed to be well liked. They had a pretty good level of chemistry and trust. She didn't tend to micromanage them, but kept a close eye on the numbers at all times and was quick to pick up the phone if she sensed something was wrong. Now, she couldn't put her finger on it, but she didn't feel confident about their momentum. Except for Jose's group, which seemed full of enthusiasm, she just didn't sense a winning spirit among the team.

Not sure what to do next, Jessica called her friend and mentor, Pat, for some advice.

Wednesday, March 6, 12:15 p.m.
Lunch With Pat

After listening to Jessica's concerns, Pat suggested it might be a motivation issue. Jessica had her doubts; she always thought that motivation was not much of an issue in a sales job. After all, a major part of her salespeople's income was from commission. They wouldn't have taken a sales job if they didn't value the money they could make, and the measures of performance were clear and easy to track. She also believed that all wanted to do a good job, and they were certainly only going to make significant commissions if they did. What else was there to diagnose?

Pat encouraged Jessica to think more broadly about the situation. Jessica said she would give that some thought.

Chapter 5

Planning a Motivation Improvement Project

How can a manager, a consultant, or an individual begin to improve motivation? Using what we understand about motivation, we first diagnose problems and opportunities in the current situation and then determine appropriate solutions. We can do this for a work group or for a single individual. Unlike the car analogy where very little is known about why the car won't start, we have now learned quite a bit about how the motivation process works and can identify the likely source of a problem.

Motivation can be diagnosed and improved informally, or you may need to organize a larger scale effort to achieve your goals. A suggested approach is to define the project in four steps:

1. Plan the project.
2. Investigate the strength of each connection and possible causes of low connections.
3. Identify appropriate solutions.
4. Decide which problem and solution to tackle and measure results.

Step 1: Plan the Project

Before starting the diagnosis, you will need to answer some initial questions. The answers to these questions will guide the rest of the effort.

Unit Size

The first question is the size of the organizational unit to diagnose. Trying to diagnose the motivation of the whole organization is not typically practical or meaningful. Because so much of motivation is under the control of the immediate supervisor, there will usually be large differences in the motivation of different units. So trying to get an overall picture of motivation both is difficult and obscures important variations in different work units.

The best approach is usually to focus on one unit at a time. A "unit" here means a group with a common mission, with one—or at the most two—levels of supervision, and where unit members have direct contact with one another on a regular basis. This would be the lowest level box on an organization chart and usually ranges from 5 to 50 people.

Diagnose the Group, Individuals, or Both?

The next question is whether the diagnosis will be done for everyone in the unit as a whole, for each person individually, for only specific individuals, or for any combination of these. If the overall level of motivation is high and only a few subordinates show low motivation, it might be better to focus on just those individuals. If the unit as a whole shows low motivation, diagnosing the unit as a whole is the best strategy to start with, possibly supplementing with individual diagnoses at a later time.

It is also quite common for the manager not to have an accurate understanding of the level of motivation in the unit. If you don't have other units with which to compare, it is hard to get a sense of the level of motivation. In this case, start with the diagnosis of the whole unit.

Another situation where the unit level diagnosis is useful is where things are going well, but the manager wants to see where there might be room for improvement. If this is the goal, start with the diagnosis of the whole unit.

Current Level of Motivation

Another issue to consider before starting the diagnosis is the current level of motivation. As noted above, it is sometimes difficult to make that judgment. As an aid to doing this, go back to the questionnaire showing symptoms of low motivation we presented at the end of chapter 1 (Table 1.1).

The symptoms of high motivation are the opposite of these. Clues to low motivation surface in ways other than just low effort. Signs of low motivation include resistance to new ideas, negative attitudes, stress symptoms, and uncooperative behaviors.

When assessing overall motivation, the accuracy of the assessment depends on the quality of the information used. It is not uncommon for individuals or groups to get a reputation for the negative or positive motivation characteristics on the list. Sometimes this reputation is justified; other times it is not. Make sure you are using accurate information to make the overall assessment, not just reputation or rumor. Identifying the overall level of motivation will provide insight into the relative difficulty of the assessment and the potential for change.

Value of the Diagnosis

To assess the potential value of making improvements, ask yourself:

- What are the important outputs (results) of the group/individual's work?
- How much of this output is currently being produced?
- How good is that amount of output compared with target performance?
- How much more valuable would a larger amount of output be?
- What is the cost of not performing to target?

The answers to these questions will provide the data to help justify the time and resources spent addressing motivation. Check your analysis with others—particularly with your boss and other work groups that rely on your group's output. You should now have a business case that you can use to communicate the rationale for the project, as well as at least one way to consider measuring the success of any changes that occur.

Set Timeline Expectations

As you will see in the following chapters, making a good diagnosis is a complex process. It will take some time to do it all. Spreading the effort over time allows for reflection, absorption of new ideas, and more buy-in to eventual changes. Moving forward faster than the group can absorb will make the process less accurate and less effective.

Step 2: Investigate the Strength of Each Connection and Possible Causes

Motivation diagnosis focuses primarily on the *connections* in the model. To do this, we will look at each connection in the following four chapters. The manager or consultant will observe, think about, and talk with the individuals involved to evaluate the strength of the connection and explore why the connection is strong or weak. Each chapter features:

- *Examples* that illustrate common situations.
- An explanation of *determinants*, the factors that are the reason for the strength of a connection.
- Additional *diagnosis considerations* including techniques and issues particular to each connection.
- A table that provides a *roadmap* for diagnosis.

Gathering Data

The two methods used in the motivation diagnosis are (1) observing and (2) gathering information from or with others.

Observing means first paying attention to what is happening. This means watching what people do, what they say, and how they act. Approach this with an open mind and simply observe. The material in the next chapters will tell you what to look for, but the attitude you have when you start this observation process is important. It is all too easy to have preconceived views of how things are or of what subordinates think. Many of these views may be accurate, but some important ones may be wrong.

This leads to the second method: gathering information from or with others. This could be through some sort of questionnaire, but more commonly it is simple face-to-face discussions. You can gather some very useful information by observation, but it is critical to verify it in discussions with subordinates and others with whom they interact. Having these diagnostic discussions is somewhat of an art. To do it in a way that produces useful information is not always easy.

Diagnosis requires a combination of observation
and discussion with others.

The biggest issue is usually reluctance on the part of subordinates. Asking questions about motivation is a loaded issue. It can easily come across as a threat to subordinates. It can sound like you are criticizing them for not being more motivated and demanding that they work harder or change in some other way. This will not go over well. Subordinates will respond with defensiveness, resentment, and anger and will usually be very hesitant to give useful information. If they do get defensive, they will also try to convince you they are highly motivated and will tend to put the blame for any problems on someone or something other than themselves.

Another problem in getting good information is that many motivation problems can be attributed to how the supervisor treats his or her people. If you are the supervisor, it will often be difficult for subordinates to tell you where they have problems with your supervision. In this situation, a questionnaire or a person outside the unit can be helpful to add to the diagnosis.

Therefore, one approach to making the diagnosis is using outside help. The process we (the authors) use to diagnose motivational issues is described in appendix 1.

An example of using outside help to diagnose motivation is shown in Appendix 1.

Introducing the Project to a Group or Individual

Properly introducing the project will go a long way toward a successful result.

1. Communicate the value of the motivation analysis by explaining *why* it is worth doing. What are the advantages of high motivation to both the people in the unit and to the organization?
2. Emphasize that the purpose is to improve, not to punish.
3. Emphasize that people in the unit will be participating throughout the project.
4. Specify how the information collected will be used in each part of the project.
5. Highlight the potential benefits of the analysis to the individuals involved: the "What's in It for Me." Focus especially on how painful it is to work in a situation of low motivation.

Remember the basic principles about people we presented early in the book, especially that people want to be respected, to have control, and to be appreciated. Try to make this diagnosis a joint effort done with the people in the unit having the dual goals of removing roadblocks to high performance and making a better place to work.

Finally, people want to do a good job. There is an innate, natural desire to be effective at what we do. This desire to do a good job is frequently driven out of people by how they are treated at work. Your job is to collaborate with the people you manage to identify and then change the factors that can bring back that natural desire.

Step 3: Identify Appropriate Solutions

Appropriate solutions use the fewest resources necessary to address the issue and avoid creating other issues. Chapter 10 deals with identified motivation problems and possible solutions.

Step 4: Decide Which Problem and Solution to Tackle and Measure Results

Change requires time, energy, and other scarce resources. One strategy is to pick a change that is likely to make the biggest difference. Another strategy is to start on one or two very small changes that will be easy to make. In both cases, success will create more enthusiasm for making more improvements.

Measurement should include:

1. Evidence of the problem before beginning the diagnosis
2. Status immediately after implementing a solution
3. Status a period of time after implementation
4. Re-evaluation one year later

Key Points

- A well-planned motivation improvement project will give you the highest chance of successfully improving motivation.
- Whether you choose to do a formal project or an informal one, there are key decisions to be made about the scope of the diagnosis including decisions on unit size, group or individual focus, current level of motivation, value of the diagnosis, and setting timelines.
- How you introduce the project to the unit is critical for success.
- Diagnosis focuses on connections and determinants of the connections.
- Appropriate solutions take difficulty level, resource limits, and unintended impacts into account.
- Plans should include measurement of success and re-evaluation.

Extended Case: Part 2

Thursday, March 7, 9:45 p.m.
at Home on Her Laptop

Pat had encouraged Jessica to think more broadly about her situation. The first question Jessica decided to pursue was whether she was facing a motivation issue or something else. She completed the 1-minute assessment questionnaire from chapter 1 for her sales force and came up with the evaluation shown in Table 5.1.

The results surprised her. She hadn't thought that things were that bad, but when she looked at each symptom, she couldn't deny some problems. It wasn't just one individual or one group; she saw these things across the board. She would have to look at the entire regional sales force. She typed out the pros and cons.

Pros	Cons
Loyal	Avoid difficult and extra work
Timely, responsible	Take convincing to try new things
Work well together	Common to complain and wait for management to fix things when broken

When she looked at the picture of the motivation model Pat had shown her and wrote out the things her sales force did, she produced the list shown in Figure 5.1.

Writing it out made it sound simple, but she knew it was all easier said than done. Lots of hours on the road, rejections, endless issues to resolve, and each month the goals were higher than the last. She remembered it well from her own days as a salesperson. The desire to do the job well came from within,

Table 5.1. Completed Motivation Symptoms Questionnaire: Do You Have a Motivation Problem?

Rarely or never	*Sometimes*	*Often*	*Do you or the people in your group…*
		×	Avoid unpleasant tasks
		×	Work inefficiently and do not want to become more efficient
	×		Focus on following rules rather than the best way to get the work done
		×	Resist new ideas and new ways of doing things
		×	Generate few innovative ideas
		×	Put in the least possible amount of effort
		×	Avoid taking on additional work
×			Avoid work—arriving late, leaving early, prolonged breaks or lunches, excessive Internet surfing, absenteeism
×			Not put in the effort in to finish work properly
	×		Give up on difficult tasks
	×		Lack enthusiasm for the work
	×		Have low job satisfaction
×			Have little loyalty to the unit or the organization
×			Have low commitment to the goals of the unit or organization
×			Frequntly report stress
×			Frequently report of fatigue
×			Have chronic physical problems (fatigue, migraines, lower back pain, trouble sleeping)
×			Show a lack of cooperation with co-workers
	×		Have frequent complaints about management and co-workers
	×		Blame others for problems
		×	Frequently complain about seemingly small issues
8	12	21	Subtotals
41	**Total Score**		

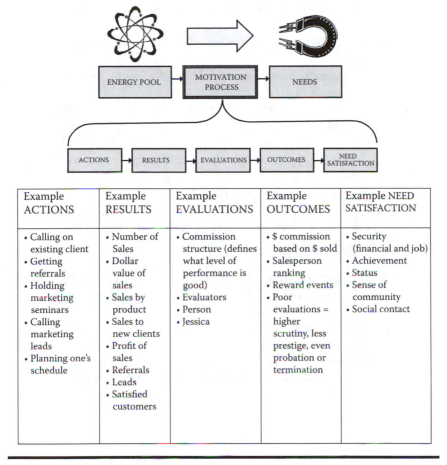

Example ACTIONS	Example RESULTS	Example EVALUATIONS	Example OUTCOMES	Example NEED SATISFACTION
• Calling on existing client • Getting referrals • Holding marketing seminars • Calling marketing leads • Planning one's schedule	• Number of Sales • Dollar value of sales • Sales by product • Sales to new clients • Profit of sales • Referrals • Leads • Satisfied customers	• Commission structure (defines what level of performance is good) • Evaluators • Person • Jessica	• $ commission based on $ sold • Salesperson ranking • Reward events • Poor evaluations = higher scrutiny, less prestige, even probation or termination	• Security (financial and job) • Achievement • Status • Sense of community • Social contact

Figure 5.1. Jessica's initial assessment.

but part of the reason she became national sales manager was to keep the sales force positive and directed. She tried to keep them from being caught up in distractions of company life with its variety of marketing, compliance, service, and financial considerations all vying for focus.

Despite her efforts, it did seem that there was a motivation problem. Jessica looked at the questions Pat had written down (see Value of the Diagnosis, chapter 5):

- *What are the important outputs of the individual/ group's work?*
- *What is the cost of not meeting the national sales goal?*
- *How much more valuable would a larger amount of output be?*

"For our group these are easy," she had told Pat. "We're salespeople, we work on commission, plus some premium for our management responsibilities." Pat suggested that there might be more to it than that. "Somewhere, something is broken. Diagnose it and see what you find."

Jessica decided that she would diagnose what was going on. Her plan was simple (see Step 1: Plan the Project, chapter 5):

1. *We are not meeting sales goals. On our current trajectory, we will be $50 million below target by the end of the year.*
2. *Our current motivation score of 41 shows that a motivation problem is contributing to the gap.*
3. *We will diagnose each regional sales force over the next 30 days and determine a course of action.*

Chapter 6

Diagnosing Action-to-Results Connections

Remember that motivation diagnosis is primarily about diagnosing the connections. To diagnose, we need three things:

- An understanding of the connection
- An understanding of the determinants of the connection
- A roadmap for how to gather data on the connection by observing and listening

Understanding Action-to-Results Connections

An action-to-results connection is the relationship we expect between how much energy we put into an action and how much of the result is generated. It is the degree to which we believe we can control our results by changing the amount of energy we apply to the actions that produce those results. Interestingly, this connection and the results-to-evaluation connection are often where connections are the weakest when there is a motivation problem, yet they are the two connections a supervisor can most easily change.

The following three examples illustrate common issues in action-to-results connections.

Example 1

The graphs in the top row of Figure 6.1 represent perceived connections for three technicians doing preventive maintenance on complex equipment. Assume that maintaining the machines is one of the major results the technicians need to produce. The horizontal axis is level of effort, ranging from a low of 0 to a high of 10. The result is the number of machines for which maintenance has been completed. Assume that each technician has 10 machines to maintain.

The graph on the left shows that if this technician puts 5 units of effort into maintenance, all 10 machines will be finished. This would be the perceived connection for a highly skilled technician who works quickly: little effort is required to finish the work. In fact, putting in more than 5 units of effort doesn't add anything, as shown by the flat slope of the function after 5 units of effort.

The technician in the right-hand figure requires 2 units of effort to finish each machine; even with 10 units of effort, only 5 of the 10 machines are finished. The middle graph shows an action-to-results connection in which the technician believes that it takes 10 units of effort to do 10 machines.

Remember, we are assuming that all three of the technicians are accurate in their perceptions. That is, the first one can do all 10 of the machines with 5 units of effort, the second with 10 units; the one on the right requires 10 units of effort to do only 5 machines.

These perceived connections influence how each technician allocates effort to actions. If 10 machines need maintenance, each of the technicians will put a different level of effort into the work. This can lead to conflicts and misunderstandings. The technician who does the maintenance quickly may not understand why co-workers are unwilling to take on more work. The slowest technician may believe that she or he is more careful and does not understand the pressure from the manager to work faster.

Example 2

The bottom row of graphs shows another example of different perceptions of action-to-results connections. In this example, two teachers differ from one another and from their principal in perceived action-to-results connections. Suppose two teachers have to submit a monthly report on each of their students. Assume that this is a fairly routine task that the teachers can readily do, and that the functions

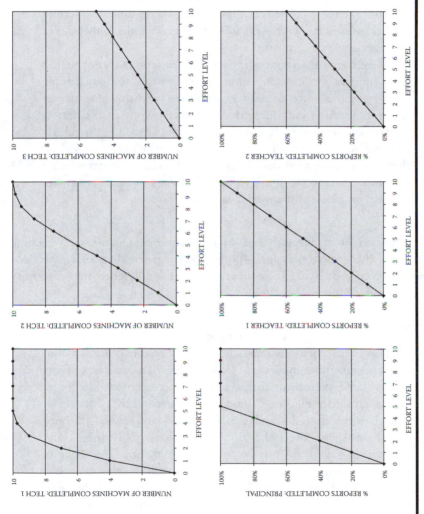

Figure 6.1.   Different action-to-results connections for different people.

for each person are linear; the connections are straight lines. The connection on the left is how the principal perceives the action-to-results connection; the principal believes that all the reports can be finished if the teachers put in a moderate amount of effort. This is shown by the steep line that gets to 100% completion if the teacher puts in 5 units of effort.

The teacher represented by the middle graph believes that it takes 10 units of effort to get all the reports finished on time. The second teacher believes that even with a lot of effort (10 units) only 60% of the reports will be completed.

The principal does not understand why the reports are not getting done and teachers are complaining that they take too much time. Identifying the action-to-results connections reveals the source of the problem. After examining these connections and their determinants, the principal may conclude that (1) he or she has unrealistic expectations, (2) the teachers may be putting much more effort into the reports than is needed, or (3) some teachers have a better strategy than others for producing the report. What the principal needs to do depends on which of these explanations is correct.

The important managerial issue in both the maintenance and teaching examples is that people may have quite different perceptions of connections between actions and results. These differences lead to differences in the quantity and quality of the results they produce.

Example 3

Suppose that Tom, a sales representative for a pharmaceutical manufacturer, sometimes makes cold calls to physicians' offices, arriving without an appointment to make a sales presentation. The graph on the left side of Figure 6.2 shows the connection that Tom *thinks* exists between effort devoted to cold calls and sales results. The horizontal axis shows levels of effort from 0 (none) to 10 (high), and the vertical axis shows number of sales per month. Tom believes that more effort devoted to cold calls will result in more sales each month. This is shown by the linear section of the function between 0 units of effort and 6 units of effort. The more effort he exerts, the more sales he makes. Tom also believes that after 6 units of effort per month, the expected number of sales per added unit of effort increases much more slowly. In other words, he believes that 6 units of effort is the point of diminishing returns for cold calls.

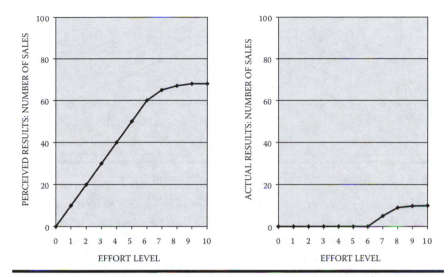

Figure 6.2. Perceived and actual action-to-results connections.

The graph on the right is the actual action-to-results connection. Based on years of experience, Tom's manager knows that cold calls rarely lead to sales. The flat section of the connection from 0 to 6 units of effort indicates that Tom can put a fair amount of effort into cold calls and get no sales at all. In fact, he must put in a great deal of effort to get even a few sales.

Determinants of Action-to-Results Connections

In the motivation diagnosis, the first step will be to assess the connections directly. That is, what *is* the perceived relationship between effort and important results? We will have more to say on how to do this below. However, if there is a problem with a connection, the next step is to look at the determinants of that connection. It is these determinants that will tell us *why* the connection is low and lead to understanding what to do to fix things. The determinants for the action-to-results connection, as shown in Figure 6.3, are capabilities, resources, authority, and work strategies.

Capabilities

We cannot act beyond our abilities. The more ability we have, the easier it is for us to translate effort into results, which produces high action-to-results con-

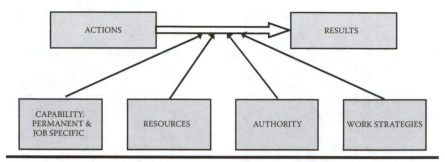

Figure 6.3.   Determinants of action-to-results connections.

nections. One type of capability is basic, *permanent ability*, which varies considerably from person to person. Some people have excellent three-dimensional visualization, abstract reasoning skills, or eye–hand coordination, while others do not. These basic abilities are essentially permanent. For practical purposes, this means that a manager cannot change them.

A second type of capability is *ability specific to the job*. Examples are how an administrative assistant keeps records in the organization's information system, how attorneys treat their firm's clients, and how technicians use a new computer-assisted robotic assembler. This type of capability is based on training and experience and, compared with permanent abilities, is much easier for the manager to change.

There is also a difference between our *actual* capabilities and what we *think* our capabilities are. What we think may or may not coincide with reality. A subordinate may think he is a good public speaker, but in fact he is not. Another subordinate may think she does not write clearly when in fact people understand what she writes quite easily.

> *What we think our capabilities are influences motivation.*
> *What our capabilities actually are influences results.*

If Linda doesn't believe she has the knowledge or skill to make a presentation to an important client, she will not want to put effort into it and will try to avoid doing the presentation. If Linda is actually quite capable, and she does put in the effort, her presentation could go well in spite of her doubts.

Resources

Resources include materials, tools, and information. A carpenter cannot frame a house if he does not have the lumber (materials), if the nail gun is not working well (tools), or if he does not have the latest plans (information).

> *People cannot control their results without the*
> *resources needed to produce those results.*

Resources influence our ability to do the actions needed to produce the results. They act as constraints on action-to-results connections and ultimately on motivation. Having the necessary resources is one needed condition for high motivation. Not having the resources means that putting effort into the actions either is not possible or will produce undesirable results. Not having the lumber makes framing the house impossible. Using a hammer instead of a nail gun means poorer-quality, slower work. Not having the most recent plans means having to redo work.

Not providing the necessary resources in the right amounts and at the right times has a negative effect on motivation. Assume that Sue is committed to doing a good job. In motivational terms, she believes that putting large amounts of time and effort into the work will satisfy her needs. If she doesn't have the resources, her first reaction will be frustration. Over time, she will realize that putting large amounts of effort into the work will not produce results (and the ultimate need satisfaction). Her motivation will decrease, and she will put less effort into the work.

Sue's manager may believe that she is not motivated and try to come up with incentives or rewards to improve her performance. This strategy will not work. The problem is not with the incentives and rewards (the outcomes); the problem is with the action-to-results connections. With a good diagnosis, the manager will realize this and collaborate with Sue to get the resources she needs rather than trying to add outcomes in the form of incentives.

Authority

A person may have the necessary capabilities and resources but not the authority to do the actions needed to produce good results. Suppose that Dave, a customer relations representative, is dealing with a customer who is frustrated with a video recorder that he cannot operate. Dave knows he could explain the VCR to the customer, but if he has been told by his boss not to get into technical matters, he doesn't have the authority to offer the explanation.

Lacking authority can decrease action-to-results connections and ultimately motivation. Suppose your staff members believe that doing the work in a certain way will produce better results, but they don't have the authority to do it that way. In formal terms, they cannot apply effort to the actions they think will produce the best results; the actions to which they are allowed to allocate effort produce poorer results. They will feel that there is a better way to get the results and what they have to do is inefficient. Their action-to-results connections will suffer.

Such a situation is frustrating to the people doing the work, especially if they really want to do a good job. Ultimately they will realize that the constraints they are working under mean they must put in more effort than is really needed to get the same results (and thus the same need satisfaction). This decreases motivation.

Work Strategies

For each action, there is an action-to-results connection. All the connections collectively represent the person's strategy for doing the job—the amount of effort put into which tasks, for how long, and in what order.

> *The best performer often is the person with the best strategy, not the person with the highest ability.*

Poor strategies mean low action-to-results connections: using a poor strategy to apply effort to actions will not produce high results. This is frustrating and over time will lead to substantial reductions in effort. If Tom believes that cold calls will lead to sales, he will put significant effort into them. When it is clear that his sales are low, frustration will follow because a lot of effort leads to little result. If his manager is critical of his sales output, this will be even more frustrating. If nothing changes, Tom keeps directing effort to cold calls, and his motivation decreases. He is using a poor strategy and over time his motivation for the whole job will decrease.

Tom's manager needs to consider the possible reasons for Tom's poor performance. She should ask about Tom's strategy, realize all the effort that is going into cold calls, and tell Tom to use a different strategy. In doing that, the manager *changes* Tom's perceived connection between cold calls and sales. Tom then allocates less effort to cold calls and puts more effort into a strategy that will produce more sales.

If Tom believes cold calls result in sales, he will put a significant amount of effort into cold calls, but not many sales will result. The sales manager sees that Tom is not making many sales and may conclude that Tom is not putting in enough effort or does not have sufficient sales ability—but neither explanation is correct. Tom is putting too much effort into cold calls. He should put more effort into fewer total calls, but take the time to set up appointments with the physicians beforehand. The problem is the *direction* of his actions, not the *amount of effort* or his *ability*. A careful analysis reveals that the problem is inaccurate action-to-results connections.

Consequently, changing work strategy is one of the most common ways to improve motivation. The best source of good work strategy may be the boss, but most often it is co-workers. Group discussions of strategy can help identify strategies that don't work and harness the accumulated knowledge and experience of the group to develop better strategies.

The best source for good work strategies is often peers, not the boss.

By understanding the accuracy of your subordinates' action-to-results connections, you can correct perceptions where needed and improve motivation.

Action-to-Results Diagnosis Roadmap

With this understanding of action-to-results connections and their determinants, we now turn to the question of how to start the action-to-results diagnosis. As a first step, focus on three to eight major results the unit is expected to produce. For a manufacturing unit, the list would probably be something like quantity of output, quality of output, working safely, meeting production schedules, doing preventive maintenance, and keeping accurate records. For a customer service unit, the major results probably would include number of customers served, customer satisfaction, completing reports on time, and errors made.

Start with the three to eight major results the person or unit is producing.

Once you identify the major results, focus on the actions that produce them. As you do this, either through observation or through discussions with your subordinates, you may need to look at smaller results and actions to pinpoint the problem. For example, if the problem is quality of output, what are the specific aspects of quality that need attention and what are the actions that produce them?

Table 6.1 provides a quick guide to diagnosing the action-to-results connections and their determinants. It describes what you should be looking for, questions to ask, and what to listen for.

Table 6.1. Diagnosis Roadmap: Action-to-Results

Definition: An action-to-results connection is the relationship we expect between how much energy we put into an action and how much of the result is generated. It is the degree to which we believe we can control our results by changing the amount of energy we apply to the actions that produce those results. Taken together, the action-to-results connections can be thought of as a person's work strategy, his or her production system for translating effort into results.

Considerations:
1. Many small results usually are combined through added effort to produce larger results. How detailed should you get? There is no clear answer. Start with the major results the person or unit is expected to produce. If the action-to-results connections are in good condition for the major results, they are probably in good condition for the smaller results as well.
2. Individual perceptions of action-to-results connections differ greatly and may or may not be accurate. They may not be the same as yours.

Diagnosing the connection: How strong are the action-to-results connections?

What	How	Listen
Identify the three to eight major results the unit is expected to produce.	• Ask your subordinates to list and rank the most important three to eight things the unit needs to do and compare them to your own list. It is surprising how often there are significant differences in the lists. Doing this exercise with your boss can also be instructive.	• Pay attention to how well the lists agree with your ideas of importance and whether there is disagreement between unit members. Discuss these differences, trying to achieve a consensus that accurately reflects importance to the organization.
Diagnose the connection for each result.	For each result, ask unit members: • Can they change the amount or quality of their result by changing the effort they put into actions?	• The more someone believes that his or her actions change the result, the stronger the action-to-results connection for that result.

—continued

Table 6.1. Diagnosis Roadmap: Action-to-Results (*continued*)

Diagnosing the connection: How strong are the action-to-results connections?		
What	*How*	*Listen*
Diagnose the connection for each result.	• Can they change the level of the result by applying energy to different actions (direction), by applying more energy (effort), or by applying energy over a longer time (persistence)? • What would happen if someone put more effort into the action? • Would that produce more of the desired result? • What would happen if someone put less effort into the action?	• Many connections are not linear. Pay special attention to points of diminishing returns. • Do all results have a strong connection, or are some strong while others are weak? • Is there a difference between your perception and the individual/unit's? How can you determine which perceptions are more accurate?

Diagnosing the Determinants: Why is a connection particularly weak or strong? What could explain what you are seeing and hearing?			
Capabilities	*Resources*	*Authority*	*Work Strategies*
Does the person have hte basic ability to do the job? Does the person have the specific training and experience neeed? Does s/he have an accurate perception of these abilities?	Does the person have the materials, tools, and information needed?	Does the person believe s/he has the authority to do what s/he thinks should be done to achieve the result?	Exactly what does the person do to achieve the result? Is the work strategy effective? Get detailed facts from them; don't assume that you already know how they get their results.

Extended Case: Part 3

Monday, March 11, 11 a.m.
Phone Meeting

On Monday, Jessica called a meeting of the regional managers and shared her thinking: "I don't like to tell you how to run your region, but we're going to have examine what's working and what's not in order to improve. This is something we'll do together. You are a talented team and you have my confidence. I hope we will get some new ideas over the next 30 days. It's going to require collecting some data. We know what our sales are today. If sales are back on track when we're done with this diagnosis and made some changes, we will have succeeded. If we are successful, it will mean dollars back in people's checks and the pride and admiration of the rest of the company. Not to mention our top salespeople's trip to Bermuda."

Jose suggested, "What kind of sales are we talking about? I personally believe we should focus sales efforts on existing customers. It is much easier to sell to an existing customer than to acquire a new one."

"That's fine if you have a big customer base, but we're trying to aggressively develop new large customers and lure them from competitors," added Susan.

"Fewer larger deals is the key to success," Dave countered. Marius just listened. The group was trying to identify the important results.

Well, Jessica thought, at least there's not silence. "Those are all good points. What if we said that our most important results are
- *retaining existing clients and*
- *attracting new profitable clients*
- *to increase dollars sold.*

Does our sales force believe that putting more effort into its work will produce more of these three results?" She was trying to get a sense of the action-

to-results connection for these three results. There was general agreement. "Can you change the level of the result by doing things differently or more persistently? If someone put more effort into retaining existing clients, for example, would this retain more clients? If you put less effort into existing clients, will they leave?" These are good ways to get a general sense of the action-to-results connections.

There was general agreement that salespeople's actions made a major difference for these results; that is, the action-to-results connections were high. Individual work strategies jumped out as the main difference in sales results.

Just to make sure, Jessica asked the managers to answer the following for each salesperson in their team (see Table 6.1: Diagnosis Roadmap: Action-to-Results).

- *Is the person capable? Is there a lack of skill or confidence? (On a scale of 1–5, with 5 being the highest.)*
- *Does the person have necessary resources? Missing information? Bottlenecked resources?*
- *Does the person feel authorized to run his or her business, or is he or she waiting for direction?*
- *Is the work strategy effective considering how much effort is being put in, on what tasks, in what order to achieve the result?*

They would also take a general sales survey that asked people about training, resources, and authority as well as anything else getting in the way of selling. The managers were fine with this, as long as it didn't encourage complaining. Jessica offered to send a memo with the general survey that would send a balanced message. "I would also like you to send me two lists—exactly what your most effective sales people do and what your least effective salespeople do. Be prepared to talk about the differences."

Thursday, March 14, 3 p.m.
in the Office

A few days later, Jessica looked through the results. Each region had at least one person with capabilities rated lower than 3, except for Jose's region where there had been a particularly effective focus on recruiting and training. Marius's had four people with capabilities rated below 3, which concerned her. Maybe he was being a hard grader? The other results of the survey were largely as expected, with one exception. Salespeople responded very minimally to questions about scheduling sales calls. Interesting. She would have to look into that one.

Next she looked at the lists of what managers observed about how the best and worst salespeople handled their jobs.

Jessica put the lists together (Table 6.2) and gave them to the group. She asked, "What do you see that is similar about the best salespeople across the regions?" The group identified personal character qualities and being organized as the two most important commonalities. There was some debate about personal qualities, and the group agreed to focus on just those areas that everyone could improve, regardless of personality. This was an example of focusing on work strategies.

It was apparent that not everyone was using the same strategy and that some strategies were more effective than others. In terms of the motivation model, changing people's work strategy is an example of changing action-to-results connections. If someone is using a strategy that is not effective, putting in high levels of effort will not produce the sales results that are desired, leading to a decrease in motivation.

Jose's specific description helped the group to clarify a key strategy on which they could all agree: schedule six weeks ahead at least 10 appointments per week with high producers. Doing this required planning a schedule as well as thinking about who the

Table 6.2. Comparison of Best and Worst Performers

West (Jose)	East (Dave)
Best:	**Best:**
Very organized—schedules 6 weeks out, keeps calendar of all appointments, to-do list of all outstanding items, meets with assistant every morning	Easy to work with
Can-do attitude—does not allow obstacles to derail his focus, reschedules, asks for help	Keeps accurate records
Lots of productive visits—at least 10 high producer visits per week	Creative
Recruits others—recognizes talent in the marketplace and gives leads to recruiters	Longstanding relationships
Worst:	**Worst:**
Face time without impact—shows up, many cancellations, inadequate materials	Too slick for own good
Few appointments—works on the fly, drops by without appointments	Does minimum
Sloppy paperwork—12 corrections needed to documents in past 30 days	Poor time management
Excuses—Always has a reason but projects or requests fall through the cracks	
Midwest (Susan)	South (Marius)
Best:	**Best:**
Track record of accomplishment	Well liked
Leader—volunteers, active in industry	Good role model
	Works hard
Worst:	**Worst:**
Negative attitude—looks only at problems in products and how we sell them	Focuses on small opportunities
Analysis paralysis—gets caught up in complexities instead of just making the sale	Hard to reach
	Always wants higher commission rate

high producers were. Additionally, if the calendar was set in advance, assistants could help those who were less organized to be prepared with materials. Managers would also be able to provide coaching in advance and see any emerging trends.

Jessica summarized for the group that the desired action would be scheduling 6 weeks out at least 10 appointments per week with high producers, and that the result would be at least 40 planned high producer meetings per month. This would likely lead to higher sales opportunity.

It made common sense, but most regions were not averaging even close to those numbers of client appointments. Only Jose's group in the West was close to this, but she didn't have very good numbers to know for sure. She asked the group to take a measurement of (a) how many weeks out sales calls were being scheduled, and (b) how many appointments with high producers were being made. This would give the group a baseline from which to measure, and validate their assumptions about best and worst performers. If the data validated their assumptions, she wouldn't wait to make this change, but would try it as soon as they had determined the baseline. This new work strategy might be a way to improve the action-to-results connection.

Chapter 7

Diagnosing Results-to-Evaluation Connections

As with the last chapter, to make the diagnosis, we need an understanding of the results-to-evaluation connection, an understanding of its determinants, and a roadmap for gathering data through observation and listening.

Understanding Results-to-Evaluation Connections

A results-to-evaluation connection is the relationship between the amount of a result that is produced and the favorableness of the evaluation by a given evaluator.

You can also think of results-to-evaluation connections as the *measurement and evaluation system*. They define what is measured and how these measures are converted into evaluations.

Example

The example in Figure 7.1 shows an accounting firm's billable hours; the result, on the horizontal axis, ranges from 25 to 50 hours per week. The vertical axis shows the level of evaluation, going from a very negative –10 through a neutral value of 0 to a very positive +10.

Averaging 25 billable hours per week gets a very negative evaluation. As the number of billable hours increases, the evaluation becomes much less negative. Averaging 33 billable hours gets an evaluation of 0; it is adequate—neither positive nor negative.

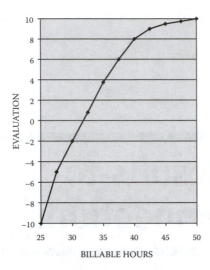

Figure 7.1. Results-to-evaluation connection.

As the billable hours increase to 40, the evaluation becomes very positive. Beyond 40, improvements in the evaluation get smaller and smaller. At the point of diminishing returns, the accountant may suffer burnout, which would reduce the level of future billable hours, or his or her fatigue may be too high to produce good client satisfaction.

Which Results Are Measured and Evaluated?

People generate many different results on the job. Some of these results are valuable to the organization, some are negative, and some are irrelevant. People measure and then evaluate the results they believe are valuable, either to themselves or to the organization.

What determines which results are measured? Remember, we make a distinction between measures and evaluations. Measures are indices of output; evaluations are formed by deciding how good or bad the result/output is. Examples of evaluations include how good or bad the number of new product ideas, the number of hours billed, or the number of missed meetings. This evaluation is essentially comparing results to a standard. Table 7.1 gives some examples of measurement (how much) and evaluation (how good).

The term *evaluation* refers here to all types of evaluations, not just formal evaluations such as annual performance reviews. In the motivation model, evaluations include feedback a person gets from the work itself, the management information system, other units in the organization, customers, family, and a person's own evaluation of his or her results.

Table 7.1. Measures and Evaluations

Measurements: "How much"	Evaluations: "How good"
I hit the ball 250 yards down the middle of the fairway.	I hit a great drive.
It took me 6 shots on the 3rd hole.	I was 2 over par on the 3rd hole.
The unit generated $457,000 in revenues this month.	We exceeded our revenue goals for the month by $57,000.
We filled 93% of the orders for the week.	Meeting orders for this week was a bit below where we want to be.
Customer satisfaction ratings show that 81% of the customers are either quite satisfied or very satisfied.	We are doing OK in customer satisfaction, but not great.
Tom misses about 25% of our staff meetings.	Tom misses too many meetings.

When you notice the work of a colleague and think it is well done or not so well done, you have made an informal evaluation.

Simultaneous Measurement and Evaluation

Although the measurement and evaluation processes are logically different, they commonly occur almost simultaneously. You watch a subordinate make a presentation to a client and conclude that she did a great job. You may not even be aware of measuring and go straight to the evaluation, although to make that evaluation, you are observing (measuring) details such as how the presentation was organized, how she dealt with questions raised by the client, and the client's reaction to the presentation.

A manufacturing manager who gets a weekly report on the number of defective units knows from experience what levels are good and what levels are bad, so going from measurement to evaluation is immediate.

We use the term *performance* to mean how well a person or a unit does the work. In fact, performance is actually evaluated results.

Determinants of Results-to-Evaluation Connections

As with the action-to-results connections in the last chapter, it is important to understand the determinants of results-to-evaluation connections so that you

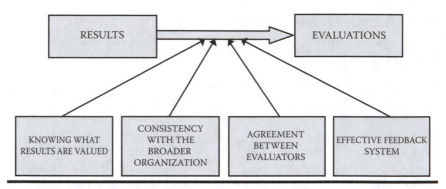

Figure 7.2. Determinants of results-to-evaluation connections.

know what causes to look for if these connections are low. The strength of the results-to-evaluation connection (Figure 7.2) is determined by (1) knowing what results are valued, (2) consistency with the broader organization, (3) agreement among evaluators, and (4) an effective feedback system.

Knowing What Results Are Valued

Managers frequently assume that their subordinates know what the important results are. This may or may not be true. Even people who have been on the job for years may have ideas different from their supervisors of what is important. It is also common for top management and middle management to have very different ideas of what the important results are.

Whether people agree on the major results is a critical issue in motivation. To maximize motivation, everyone—subordinates, supervisors, peers, internal and external clients—needs to know and agree on what the important results are.

> ***Don't assume your subordinates know what results
> are important to the organization.***

Disagreement can mean two different things here. First, there can be disagreements that everyone knows about. For example, suppose a manager wants photocopier repair technicians not only to repair their customers' photocopiers but also to sell them long-term maintenance agreements. The technicians are uncomfortable doing sales and resist attempts to get them to spend much effort on sales. This type of disagreement is clear to all.

A much more difficult situation occurs when *no one realizes* that people differ in how they see the importance of results. This is very common, even when people have worked together for years. Managers tend to assume that what is important is obvious. Subordinates may also feel they fully understand what is important. Neither group realizes that they don't agree.

The implications for motivation are clear. If people think that certain results are important, they believe that producing these results will lead to positive evaluations, which lead to positive outcomes, and eventually to need satisfaction. Conversely, results that are not seen as important will not influence evaluations, outcomes, or need satisfaction. Motivation will be strong for the important results and much lower or nonexistent for the less important results.

For example, suppose a life insurance salesperson believes that the number of sales is important but the dollar amount of the policies is not important. He will spend more effort on actions that will generate many sales and less effort on strategies that will produce high-dollar policies. If this is consistent with the organization's priorities, this is fine, but if it isn't, the salesperson is using his energy in a way that is not optimal for the organization.

A diagnosis that identifies the important results will reveal unknown lack of agreement. This can be particularly useful to do when priorities or evaluators change, such as when there is a change in higher management or in major customers.

Consistency With the Broader Organization

The evaluation system must match what is truly of value to the organization. Alignment between the unit's major results and the strategic objectives of the organization ensures that evaluations accurately define the value that is added to the organization. Results with steep result-to-evaluation connections by definition are the ones seen as adding large amounts of value to the organization.

Although this may seem obvious, it is surprising how often this sort of problem comes up. One example came from a maintenance setting. A key result measured by the unit was average time to complete repairs. This implied that taking less and less time to do the repair added value. A careful analysis revealed that what was really important was meeting the demand for repaired items, not average repair time. So if times were slow, it was better to do a more thorough repair, including some preventive maintenance. If times were busy, it was better to do the minimum needed to get the item back into operation. The measured result was changed from average repair time to percentage of demand met.

> *It takes considerable care to design an evaluation system consistent with what adds value to the organization.*

A person will tend to behave consistently with the evaluation system. The more powerfully the reward system is tied to evaluations, the more the person will behave consistently with that evaluation system. Ironically, with a mismatch between evaluations and actual value to the organization, the better the reward system, the worse things become for the organization.

> ***If the evaluation system and what adds value to the organization are different, people will act based on the evaluation system.***

This consistency diagnosis can be done by the unit, but the manager has a special responsibility. The manager usually has the best grasp of higher-level organizational objectives, so it is frequently the manager who can best determine whether the system rewards actions that are truly valuable to the organization.

Agreement Among Evaluators

Different evaluators will evaluate the same results differently. Consider the example of an accountant's billable hours and several different evaluators: the accountant's manager, her peers, her clients, and her spouse (Figure 7.3). The connection for the accountant's *manager* (upper left) shows that billable hours are very important; the slope is very steep. The result is important because variations in number of billable hours result in large variations in the evaluation.

Billable hours are important to her *peers* (upper right), as shown by the slope of the line, but not nearly as important to peers as to her manager. For peers, a successful colleague makes the firm more profitable, allowing for larger bonuses, so there is more value to peers as billable hours increase. The flattening of the line indicates that increases beyond 40 hours are of no additional value to peers. It is difficult to average more than 40 billable hours, and her peers may not want to have to try to match such a high standard. The positive of higher bonuses and the negative of higher standards cancel each other out, resulting in a flat line.

The connection for her *clients* (lower left) is flat until billable hours get above 40, when it drops. Variation in billable hours has no impact on clients unless they see that their accountant is too tired to work effectively, so very high billable hours are seen as somewhat negative by her clients.

The connection for her *spouse* (lower right) shows that increases in billable hours from 25 to 35 are seen as positive: her spouse realizes that she must produce a certain number of billable hours in order to succeed in the firm. Hours in the 35 to 40 range begin to encroach on the amount of time available for home activities. The net effect is essentially the same evaluation for different numbers of billable hours in this range. When the hours rise above 40, her spouse's evaluation starts to become very negative because she spends so much time at work and is exhausted when she gets home.

Thus, different evaluators have different connections, and these differences can be large. This is called *role conflict*. Role conflict produces anxiety and stress, wasted energy. If different evaluators control outcomes that are important to me,

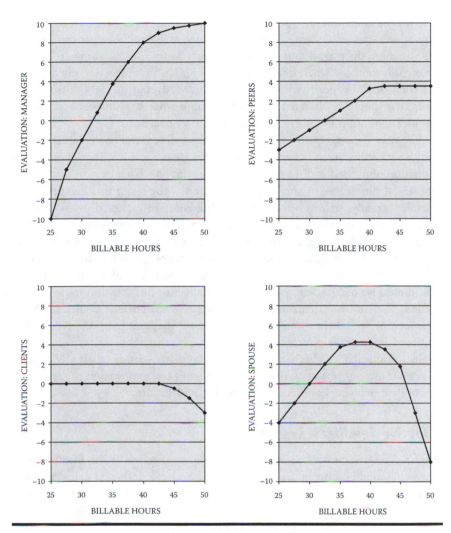

Figure 7.3.   Results-to-evaluation connections: Different evaluators.

I may feel that I can't win; pleasing one evaluator displeases another. Another consequence of role conflict is becoming secretive about output. If evaluators do not know what the outputs are, they cannot evaluate the person. If the conflict isn't resolved, I may leave the situation, either physically or psychologically. Role conflict also produces job dissatisfaction, which can lead to absenteeism and turnover because it is impossible to get highly positive evaluations from all important evaluators.

Pay special attention to role conflicts in your diagnosis.

An especially difficult type of conflict arises when a person's *own* results-to-evaluation connections are substantially different from the organization's. In this situation, the person must choose between doing what he thinks is best for the organization and what someone else thinks is best. Doing what others expect and want produces positive evaluations and rewards, but he feels he is wasting effort that should be directed elsewhere. Doing what *he* thinks is best for the organization means lower evaluations and lower rewards.

You may not realize that a subordinate has a different idea of the results-to-evaluation connections. When the differences are not known, the subordinate's evaluation of himself is different from your evaluation. This in turn can lead to substantial differences in the outcomes (rewards) the subordinate expects and what he actually gets. When there are differences in expected evaluations or rewards, both the manager and the subordinate react negatively. Your subordinate may attribute the unexpected difference to your lack of knowledge or appreciation of what he does and believe you are doing a poor job as manager. You may attribute the unexpected difference to the subordinate's being unrealistic about his contribution, never being satisfied, or not wanting to do what is needed. The reality is that none of these negative attributions is correct. What is happening is that the two of you don't realize that you have different sets of results-to-evaluation connections.

It is impossible to eliminate all of these conflicts, but discussion of results-to-evaluation connections with your subordinates and your manager goes a long way toward reducing conflict and improving motivation.

Effective Feedback System

The final determinant of results-to-evaluation connection is the feedback system—the combination of the measurement and evaluation systems. A good feedback system is essential for good motivation, and especially for good results-to-evaluation connections. It is impossible to have good results-to-evaluation connections unless the results (the measurement system) and the evaluation (the evaluation system) are accurate and clear. The feedback system is the area where the most significant improvements in motivation can usually be made. It's fairly inexpensive and can be done without additional resources, but considerable effort is required.

> *The single most important thing a manager can do to contribute to good motivation is to have a good feedback system.*

A truly effective feedback system is a complex thing. The feedback system needs to provide valid, quantitative measures of output (results) that are given to unit personnel in a formal, written way on a regular, predictable schedule. This is very different from an annual performance appraisal. Good feedback is done much more often and is custom designed to your own work unit using measures that validly reflect the results you need to generate.

A Good Feedback System Needs to Address All These Issues

Individual versus group feedback. A major issue is whether the feedback should be based on individual or group output. The most common form of individual evaluation is the formal performance appraisal, which is usually tied to raises and sometimes to promotions. Although formal evaluation has some value as feedback, it occurs too infrequently and is often too general to be useful for improving motivation.

Individual feedback often doesn't fit the work. In most jobs, people work interdependently; how good the results are depends in part on what others do, either because they are part of a team effort or because the result cannot be produced without the work of a number of different people. In this case, it is difficult to separate out what one individual has done. The whole result can be evaluated, but not the contribution of each individual.

In this situation, the feedback system should be based on the group's results, and feedback should go to the group as a whole. This type of feedback, based on the results the group produces, clarifies the results-to-evaluation connections for their work and can be given much more frequently than formal performance appraisals.

Use individual feedback when people work largely independently such as in sales or some types of service jobs. If people must work together to produce the important results, use group-based feedback.

Results-based feedback. A good feedback system focuses on results: feedback is about the specific work the unit is doing. This means developing measures tailored to your work. Results measures are the actual outputs of value to the organization: the units produced, the customers served, the reports completed on time, the number of errors made, and so forth. In contrast, many performance appraisal systems focus on *process* or *skills*. For example, planning is a process, and technical knowledge is a skill. Neither is results.

Typical performance appraisals are designed so that everyone in a broad part of the organization can be evaluated with the same instrument. Formal performance appraisals have their place, but they do not focus on results and they are done so rarely that they are not of as much value as feedback systems that will optimize motivation. So, regular performance appraisals are rarely effective ways of maximizing motivation. A good feedback system is based on measures of results specific to that unit.

Measurement of all important results. Developing a bad feedback system is easy; all you have to do is measure the things that are easy to measure. This is the most common type of feedback system. For example, it is usually easy to measure quantity but hard to measure quality. Measuring only quantity sends the message that this is the only important result. It often takes considerable effort to develop good measures of *all* the important results, but the effort is worth it.

Quantitative information. Some form of quantitative data is needed for both the manager and the subordinates to unambiguously assess performance. Qualitative information can and should be added, especially to help make performance improvements, but quantitative information is essential.

Staff members have control over measured results. If people are measured and evaluated on things over which they have no control, motivation suffers. By definition, a measure over which people do not have control is one that produces low action-to-result connections. Not being able to control the measure (the result) means the action-to-results connection is bad and leads to rapid decreases in motivation.

Understanding of the feedback system. Your subordinates must understand the feedback system. They should know (a) what results will be measured, (b) how each will be measured, (c) how the measures are to be combined, and (d) how the information is to be used.

Relative importance of results. Not all results are equally important. More precisely, not all results add value to the organization equally. Results-to-evaluation connections capture this differential importance by the relative slopes of the functions.

Valid measures, perceived as valid. To produce good motivation, the results measures you use in the feedback system must be valid and also must be *perceived* as valid. It is tempting to use measures that are readily available from the organization's information system, but they may or may not be good measures of the unit's results. Take the time to make sure the measures you use are valid and perceived as valid.

Appropriate level of specificity. Feedback needs to be specific enough to allow people to change behavior (actions) based on the feedback. If it is too general, people may know how they are doing but not know enough about what to change in order to improve. Feedback can also be too specific—too detailed. People do not know what to focus on because there is too much information. How specific to make feedback is a judgment call. However, typically 8 to 15 results measures are sufficient to capture the important results at the optimal level of specificity.

Both descriptive and evaluative information. We have made the point that the feedback system is the combination of the measurement (how much) and evaluation (how good) systems. You cannot understand the relationship in results-to-evaluation connections without both measurement (results) and evaluation. Think about getting the results of an exam—a score of 83, let's say. This is a *description* of your result, but it doesn't tell you *how well* you did. For that, you need evaluation—you need to know that 83 corresponds to a grade of B, so you know you did well, but not exceptionally well.

Acceptance of feedback system. The best feedback system will largely be useless if it is not accepted by those being evaluated. They must understand it and see it as valid and fair. Acceptance includes a number of the feedback characteristics we have already discussed, such as completeness, validity, and control over measures, but a key means to achieve acceptance is *participation* by the subordinates in designing the feedback system. Participation fosters acceptance, ownership, understanding, and belief in the validity of the system.

Fair evaluation system. Fairness essentially means that the evaluation is consistent across people and over time, so the same results get the same evaluation over time regardless of who produced the results or who does the evaluation.

Timely feedback. Feedback should be as close in time to performance as possible. Feedback given months after the work is done is not nearly as useful.

Regular, predictable feedback schedule. The feedback system must give information at regular, predictable intervals. This means a formal feedback system, usually in written form, that provides information on results frequently. If it takes less than a day to do one unit of work, weekly feedback should be used. If it takes more than a day but less than 2 to 3 weeks to do one unit of the work, monthly feedback is best. For those jobs where one unit of work takes longer, use an interval that allows for at least one cycle of work to be done. By far the most common interval for most jobs is monthly. It is important that subordinates know when to expect feedback.

Opportunity to use feedback to make improvements. For motivation to be high and for performance improvements to occur, people need to process the feedback they get. Group discussion is useful, whether the feedback is at the individual or the group level. Your goal is to foster a habit of using feedback to plan improvements. One of the best ways to improve work strategies is group discussion of feedback. Ask the group to come up with strategies to improve results; then, at the next discussion of feedback, determine whether the new strategy worked. If it did, keep using it. If not, try a new strategy.

Stable feedback system. For strong results-to-evaluation connections, the feedback system must be stable over time. This doesn't mean that it can never change—improvements and updates are sometimes necessary. What it does mean is deciding with your subordinates on a good feedback system and avoiding the flavor-of-the-month approach where what is important changes whenever a senior manager reads a new article on the latest management fad.

These feedback system characteristics are summarized in Table 7.2. Use this table for you and your subordinates to evaluate your feedback system. Get the average score from the 1 to 5 scale on each characteristic. Characteristics with

Table 7.2. Evaluating Your Feedback System

Use the following list for you and your subordinates to evaluate your feedback system.
Instructions: Evaluate the feedback system in your unit. For each item, use a rating scale: a value of 1 = Strongly Disagree, 2 = Somewhat Disagree, 3 = Neither Agree nor Disagree, 4 = Agree, or 5 = Strongly Agree.
Does the feedback system in your unit have the following characteristics?
• Use the correct unit of analysis (individual or group)
• Is based on results
• All important results are measured
• Uses quantitative measures
• Is based on measures people in the unit can control
• Is understood by the people using it
• Captures the relative importance of the different results
• Uses measures that are valid
• Uses measures that are perceived as valid
• Is based on measures at the most useful level of specificity
• Includes both descriptive and evaluative information
• Is accepted by unit personnel
• Is seen as fair by unit personnel
• Is given in a timely way
• Is done on a regular, predictable schedule
• Allows people in the unit the opportunity to plan improvements in work strategy
• Is stable over time

scores below 4.0 need attention. If you have four or more characteristics with scores below 4.0 your feedback system can be substantially improved.

Results-to-Evaluation Diagnosis Roadmap

Diagnosing the results-to-evaluation connections is the most challenging part of the motivation diagnosis. This is because results-to-evaluation connections are complex and there are many issues to address. At the same time, this is a major place where motivational improvements can be made and a place where the supervisor has considerable control over needed changes. Because of this, we will go into more detail about this part of the diagnosis.

The first step in diagnosing results-to-evaluation connections is to ask your subordinates to identify the *important evaluators*—the people who control outcomes that are important to them. You as the manager will certainly be one of the important evaluators. Each person will also be an important evaluator for himself or herself because our evaluation of our own results leads to important outcomes we give ourselves. Subordinates, peers, and customers within the organization may also be key evaluators.

Important evaluators outside the organization may be job related (customers, suppliers) or not directly related to the job (spouses, families, friends). Motivation problems on the job are sometimes attributable to evaluators off the job who control valuable outcomes. For example, an employee who has children will feel a strong desire to spend enough time with them. His children control important outcomes such as approval and believing he is a good parent. If they are unhappy with how little he is home (an evaluation), their reactions can be powerful negative outcomes for him.

Next, identify the 8 to 15 measures of your 3 to 8 results. For example, if one important result is quantity of output, what exact measures will you use to assess how well this result is being met? To do this well is a very challenging task. Work with your subordinates on this task. It is critical that good measures are developed. They must cover all of the important results, be valid and perceived as valid, be largely under the control of the unit, be available in a timely way, and be cost-effective to collect. Review existing measures for how they are collected and calculated and whether they need to be changed to meet the above criteria. It will almost always be the case that new measures must be added to cover all result areas completely. Participation is critical during this process. Be prepared for this step to take a considerable amount of time and effort.

After you identify the major evaluators and the results measures, get an overall sense of the results-to-evaluation connections for each major evaluator. Remember that you are interested in the *relationship* your staff sees between results and evaluations. The issue is what happens to the evaluation if the results measures change.

To start with, ask if doing better on each of the results measures causes the evaluation from that evaluator to go up. Ask what happens to the evaluation if the results measures get worse. These questions will provide interesting information: individuals may not know if there is an overall positive relationship between results and the evaluations of some evaluators. For example, they may not know that an internal customer evaluates some of your unit's results but not others. During this process, expect that some of the measures you have identified will need to be revised.

You may also want to do this process more formally by actually drawing the connections in the format we use here in the book. The process for doing this is described in Appendix 1.

Finding Unclear Connections

As you have these discussions, questions frequently arise about how results are evaluated. Subordinates often don't know what the acceptable level of output is, much less have a clear picture of the overall shape of the connection. This is called *role ambiguity*. It is unclear what results are important, what is expected, and what level of output is considered good and not so good. Role ambiguity is common when a person begins a new job; it is expected that things will become clear with experience. Unfortunately, it is common for this lack of clarity to go on for years. As manager, you probably have a clear idea of what most of these connections look like, but you may need to ask questions of evaluators to clarify. For motivation to be high, it is essential that you and your team become clear on what would be great, good, neutral, and poor levels of performance for each major result.

If connections are unclear, it means people do not know how their results are translated into evaluations. People cannot connect their efforts to need satisfaction if links are missing or unknown. Other negative effects of unclear connections include the stress that occurs when people do not know where to focus their efforts, and dissatisfaction when effort is wasted on what later turn out to be unimportant things. When evaluations or outcomes do not match expectations, then frustration, disappointment, and resentment will occur. Over time, motivation decreases.

Finding Frequently Changing Connections

Pay particular attention to situations where connections change frequently, or people *believe* they change frequently.

An example is rapidly changing priorities. A new push from management says that developing subordinates is the best way to build the organization; next month the push is customer satisfaction—then quality, then profitability. Each new focus means a change in results-to-evaluation connections. Whatever result is being pushed, the message is that this connection has been too flat (not important enough) and needs to be more steep (more important). The implied message is also that in the future, this result will be carefully measured, and evaluations and outcomes will be based on it. If, however, there is a new push every month, there is little reason for staff members to respond. More precisely, there is little reason for people to change how they allocate energy. To produce more of the

Table 7.3. Diagnosis Roadmap: Results-to-Evaluation

Definition: A results-to-evaluation connection is the relationship between the amount of a result that is produced and the favorableness of the evaluation. Taken together, the results-to-evaluation connections define the measurement and evaluation system.
Considerations: 1. People generate many different results. The measurement system determines which results will be measured, either formally or informally. 2. Measurement describes the amount of the result. Evaluation describes how good or bad that amount is. 3. Measurement and evaluation often happen nearly simultaneously.
Diagnosing the connection: How strong are the results-to-evaluation connections?

What	*How*	*Listen*
Identify the important evaluators. This includes your boss and yourself as well as others such as subordinates, peers, customers, family, and friends. Typically there will be 4 to 6 major evaluators. Identify what 8 to 15 measures to use for 3 to 8 major results identified in the diagnosis of action-to-results connections. What is the results-to-evaluation connection for each evaluator on each measure?	• Ask who are the people inside and outside the organization who get value from unit members' results. • Discuss the results measures that you do or should use to assess how well you are producing each result. • For each result measure, ask what level of the result each evaluator considers good, OK, and poor. • If you want a more accurate picture, follow the process described in appendix 2 for graphing a connection.	• Do unit personnel understand who all the important evaluators are? • Do you have good measures for each result? Do unit members agree they are valid measures? Are they measures the unit has substantial control over? • Is their view of what are good, OK, and poor result levels accurate? • The steeper the overall slope of the graphic, the more important that result is to that evaluator. Are the slopes they report accurate?

– continued

Table 7.3. Diagnosis Roadmap: Results-to-Evaluation (*continued*)

		• The more someone believes that different amounts of results produced mean different evaluations, the stronger the results-to-evaluation connection. • Do the connections change frequently?

Diagnosing the determinants: Why is a connection particularly weak or strong? What could explain what you are seeing and hearing?

Knowing what results are valued	*Consistency with the efficient broader organization*	*Agreement among evaluators*	*Feedback System*
Review the list of important results measures done for action-to-results connections, including the relative importance of each.	Are all these results and how they are measured consistent with what the organization truly values?	Look at the results-to-evaluation connections for different evaluators. How different are evaluations of th same result? Is it possible to get a positive result from everyone at the same time? Will success with one evaluator mean failure with another?	Use Table 7.2 to evaluate your feedback system. Identify where it can be improved.

result is not worth the trouble because the energy will be wasted when another change occurs. So, people will pay lip service to the new priority but won't reallocate energy.

Another example is high management turnover. Changing evaluators can mean changing what constitutes good and poor performance. Too many changes can leave people with uncertainty about how today's result will be evaluated tomorrow.

As with the last chapter, a Diagnosis Roadmap (Table 7.3) is offered highlighting the results-to-evaluation diagnosis process.

Extended Case: Part 4

Tuesday, March 19, 9 a.m.
Regional Meeting at Headquarters

Today was the first chance Jessica had to get the team in person around the table. The four regional managers were at headquarters for a week of performance reviews and training. They would also be able to speak with many of their salespeople. Nothing had changed yet in the field, and she knew that her managers were nervous. Indeed, they had found that sales calls were not being planned far in advance, and the new measures were not met with great enthusiasm. It was too soon to tell whether a change would make an impact.

Recalling the conversation the team had about different customer targets, Jessica suggested that her managers consider whether their salespeople knew which results were important. Knowing which are the important results improves both action-to-results and results-to-evaluation connections. So was it large customers, new customers, existing customers? What else? Jessica asked each manager to ask the salespeople about what results each of them believed were most important. She also assigned each manager to speak with a manager in the key functional areas of the company—Marketing, Com-

pliance, Service, and Accounting—to find out what results were important to them from Sales. In terms of the motivation model, Jessica identified who the important evaluators of her groups' results are. Asking her people to meet with them is her way of making these evaluators, or internal customers, more salient to her managers.

Monday, March 25, 11 a.m. Conference Call

When Jessica reconvened the team, there was a lot to report. Not only were there differences of opinion about what customers to target, there were differences of opinion about what products should be sold, how regions should work more closely together, and how salespeople needed to be part of internal redesign efforts. Compliance wanted salespeople to disclose all possible problems so that customers would not have high expectations. Service wanted salespeople to promise long lead times for delivery so there would be no rush orders. "Sales is doing a great job" meant something different to almost everyone.

Jessica wasn't surprised, but she could see that her managers were overwhelmed. "Let's try to make sense of who needs what, how well we're doing, and the implications for the organization and for sales." This is an example of identifying the important results for all the important evaluators.

The team looked at each group at a time, and came up with the details in Table 7.4.

On the topic of higher sales goals, the team became particularly animated. "Marketing and Accounting need to talk to each other. They come out with products and features they want us to sell, we have to explain it all to our customers, and in the end, selling that product or feature extensively may be unprofitable. We're working hard and we could be working against ourselves if the result is higher sales goals. This is typical of the mixed messages

Table 7.4. Different Evaluators

	Marketing	*Compliance*	*Service*	*Accounting*
Evaluate Sales on	Amount sold, product feature knowledge, selling across territory lines	Disclosing all risks, selling appropriate products, complying with regulations	Comfortable lead times for turnaround, complete transactions with all necessary information	Understanding product profitability, focus on profitable customers
How we're doing	Sales force doesn't always push featured products	Acceptable	Complaints about incomplete transactions	Too many sales of less profitable products
Implications	Marketing campaigns less effective	No changes suggested	Increase in volume of complaints puts more demand on service staff and aggravates customers	Declining profit margins push sales goals higher

from management. Not you, of course, Jess, but cor-
porate," said Dave. This is an example of a conflict
between the results-to-evaluation connections for
different evaluators.

Jessica first thought of telling them that this was
a reality they just had to accept, and ask them what
they wanted her to do about it, but she refrained.
Solving the problem of how Marketing and Accounting worked together was more than she intended to
take on. Instead, she thought for a minute and said,
"You've done a good job of finding out what results
people feel are important outside of sales, and I'll
share our findings with Luke." Luke was the division
president and the group relaxed a bit to see that their
issues were being taken seriously.

Jessica continued, "When we started diagnosing the actions of our sales force, we focused the importance of making planned sales calls, but we didn't agree on what customers or products were most important—large clients, new clients, all of the things we've talked about. I think we need to go back and understand what results we really want, knowing that what we sell has implications for the larger organization." This is an example of getting even clearer on what the important results are.

After an extended discussion, the group agreed on the following:

- Ask Accounting to provide a profitability analysis to determine the best opportunities by region
- Jess would work with the head of Accounting to approach Marketing about developing appropriate campaigns to support these efforts

Tuesday, March 26, 12:30
Lunch

The next day, Jessica had lunch with Pat again and described what the group had found so far. Pat was interested to hear about the different expectations of salespeople, managers, and others in the organization. "How do salespeople know if what they are doing is effective?"

"You mean other than a commission check each month?" asked Jessica.

"Yes, I mean other than receiving a check, how do people know how well they are doing?" Pat urged her to look at this more carefully and gave Jessica a feedback checklist (see Table 7.2) that she sent on to her managers.

Friday, March 29, 3 p.m.
Conference Call

After the initial greetings, Jess explained, "The response to our request for Accounting and Marketing support has been great. I expect we'll have some initial analysis in the next 3 to 6 weeks. This should help identify the best products to focus on and thereby clarify what results are important. In the meantime, from what you've sent to me, I'd like to congratulate you on some progress we've already made. At least 30% of the sales force now has client calls planned 6 weeks out. I also urge you to congratulate your salespeople who are doing this. Next month we'll be able to see if increased sales will follow. I want to see the number of people planning that far out increase. Until we have more information on our client and product mix, this is the most important action driving sales that we can focus on." Enthusiastic, she was about to call the meeting to a close when Jose jumped in.

"About that feedback checklist you sent?" he began, "I felt pretty good about the feedback I give in my region, but I think we should be giving more feedback in all territories. I also feel like we have put a big emphasis on service and I'd like to see some feedback from the Service group on a regular basis so I can show my people our progress." Jose suggested that an important result that has not been fully considered was service to customers. A way of measuring how well this result is being achieved is needed.

"Suggestions for action?" asked Jessica.

"I'd be willing to work with Jose on some feedback measures. I'd like to hear more about how he runs his region anyway and he uses the most metrics already," added Marius. Dave and Susan agreed to talk with Service and identify some feedback measures that could be provided monthly.

"Great!" said Jessica. "That's the spirit!"

It was great. Her managers were taking action, senior management was taking note of her strategic *focus, and the additional sales calls were bound to convert to more sales. It had been nearly 30 days and soon she would have to shift gears and focus on the National Sales Conference coming up in 8 weeks. It was the one time of year when she got to see nearly the entire sales force and she wanted to make it count.*

Chapter 8

Diagnosing Evaluation-to-Outcomes Connections

Understanding Evaluation-to-Outcome Connections

Evaluation-to-outcome connections are the perceived relationships between the levels of the evaluation and the level of the outcomes received. They define the *reward* system—how evaluators convert evaluations into outcomes. They also define expected outcomes (rewards and punishments) and the degree to which they are tied to evaluations (both formal and informal).

Before assessing your unit's understanding of the relationship between evaluations and outcomes, clarify your own understanding. This is important because your understanding may be different from your boss's, and you want to be accurate when you speak with your team—especially when it comes to rewards. Below are examples of common evaluation-to-outcome connections for compensation, recognition, and promotion.

Examples

Compensation. The graphs in Figure 8.1 show how different raise systems look as evaluation-to-outcome connections. The graph in the upper left is the evaluation-to-outcome connection for across-the-board raises. If everyone gets the same percentage pay raise, the level of the evaluation has no effect on the size

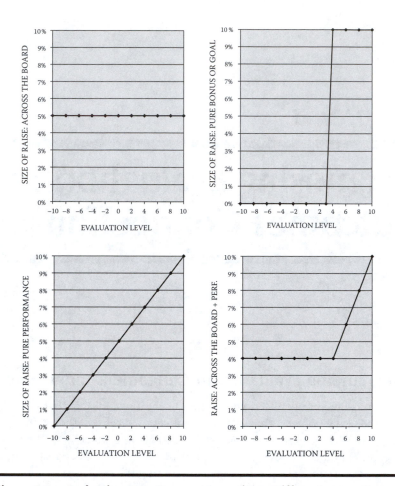

Figure 8.1. Evaluation-to-outcome connections: Different pay systems.

of the raise and the connection is flat. Raises provide no motivation for high performance. They will motivate the person to do only the minimum needed to keep the job.

The upper right graph shows the connection for raises determined entirely by a bonus or goal-setting system. The only way to get a pay raise is to get to a certain level of performance—a certain level of evaluation. At that level, the raise is the same percentage for everyone who reaches the goal. Those whose performance is higher than the goal get the same raise as those who simply meet the goal. The flat line part of the function shows a zero raise for evaluations from very low (–10) to somewhat positive (+3). Evaluations of +4 or higher trigger a 10% raise. Once the evaluation reaches 4, the line is again flat because performance higher than the goal gets the same raise as performance that just meets the goal. Raises will motivate people to get to the level of evaluation needed to get the bonus, but not to perform any higher than that.

The lower left graph shows the connection for a pay system in which raises are determined solely by performance: the level of the evaluation determines the size of the raise. Low levels of evaluation result in no raises or small ones; high levels of evaluation result in large raises. Assuming the other connections are good, such a system will motivate people to try for the highest performance possible.

Most pay systems use a combination of these methods to determine raises. For example, an across-the-board increase may be combined with a merit increase: everyone gets a cost-of-living increase, and high performers also get a merit raise. The last graph shows such a pay system. No matter what the evaluation, everyone gets at least a 4% raise. An evaluation above 4 earns a larger raise, and the raise gets larger as the evaluation gets more positive. Raises under this system will motivate people to high performance if they believe they can get the higher evaluations. If they believe it is not possible to achieve the high level of evaluation, the raise will provide no motivation to perform above the minimum needed to keep the job.

Recognition. Figure 8.2 shows connections for recognition and promotions. The upper pair of graphs is for the outcome of praise and criticism from one's manager. The vertical axes go from –5 (strong criticism) through 0 (neither criticism nor praise) to +5 (strong praise). The left-hand graph shows a very strong connection between level of the evaluation and amount of praise or criticism. Low levels of evaluation result in very strong criticism. Evaluations near zero— just meeting expectations—result in neither criticism nor praise. High positive evaluations result in high levels of praise. This is an example where people expect that the supervisor will give them clear positive and negative messages in the form of praise or criticism about how well they are doing.

On the right, the connection is a straight line. This person expects neither praise nor criticism regardless of the level of the evaluation. Some managers say nothing about performance, no matter how good or bad it is; people simply get no feedback. Some managers give random praise and criticism that are more functions of the manager's mood than a result of what the subordinate has done. From the experience of the subordinate in this example, there is no apparent connection between performance and the level of criticism or praise, and criticism and praise occur pretty much equally or never occur at all.

Promotions. The middle row of graphs in Figure 8.2 shows evaluation-to-outcome connections for promotions. The horizontal axes are the level of the evaluation and the vertical axes are the probability of getting the promotion. In the left-hand graph, there is a strong relationship between level of evaluation and chances for promotion. An evaluation below the expected level of zero offers no

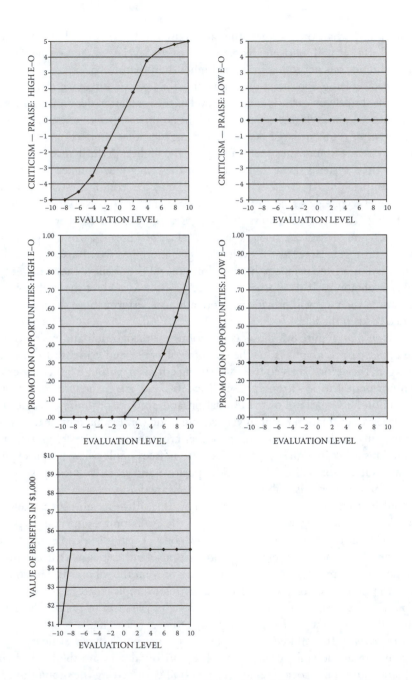

Figure 8.2. Evaluation-to-outcome connections: Different outcomes.

chance for promotion; as the evaluation level gets higher, the chances for promotion increase dramatically.

In the graph on the right, the evaluation-to-outcome connection is very low. In fact, it is flat. Chances of promotion are about one in three (0.30) no matter what the evaluation is. This type of connection characterizes a setting where promotion is determined solely by time at a certain level and availability of a new position. In time, everyone is promoted as long as there is an opening. The level of the evaluation is irrelevant.

Other Rewards. The graph in the bottom row shows an evaluation-to-outcome connection for the combined dollar value of health, dental, disability, and life insurance benefits. This outcome may not seem to be tied to evaluations at all: everyone at the same job level gets the same insurance benefits regardless of performance. But these benefits are tied to evaluations in the sense that people must stay in the organization to get them. They must produce at least a minimum level of results to keep the job. The benefits drop to zero at very low levels of evaluation, when they are asked to leave the organization.

Retirement benefits, some stock options, and the quality of the work setting are costly outcomes, and everyone at the same job level gets them more or less equally. They are not typically tied to evaluation of results. To the extent that these outcomes are valuable to people, they will motivate them to stay with the organization, which is of course important. The outcomes motivate them to perform at least well enough to keep from being fired but have no effect on motivation or performance beyond that.

> *If outcomes are not tied to a person's results and evaluations*
> *(performance), there is no reason to expect that the outcomes*
> *will motivate the person to produce more results.*

Determinants of Evaluation-to-Outcome Connections

The determinants of evaluation-to-outcome connections (Figure 8-3) are the level and number of outcomes, consistency across people and consistency over time.

Outcomes

The more outcomes that are available, the stronger overall evaluation-to-outcome connections can be. If many outcomes are available and are clearly tied to formal or informal evaluations, evaluation-to-outcome connections will be strong and will add to motivation.

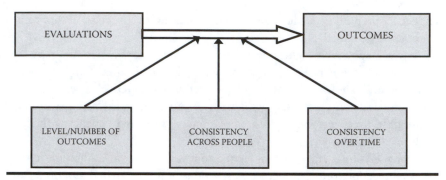

Figure 8.3. Determinants of evaluation-to-outcome connections.

Outcomes can be external or internal, formal or informal, positive or negative. Table 8.1 offers examples of outcomes to inspire you and your subordinates to think beyond the obvious ones. Go through this list, add to it, and ask how many are tied to performance (level of evaluation). Another approach is to ask what a person has to do to get each one.

Consistency

Consistency across people and over time together get at the fairness of the reward system.

Consistency across people means that two people whose performance (evaluation) is equal should get the same level of the outcome: the same raise, the same promotion opportunities, and the same recognition. Two people whose evaluations are different should get different outcomes.

Consistency over time means that evaluation levels that produced an outcome at one time should also produce it at a later time. This consistency (raises are based on the same factors again and again, for example) helps make the evaluation-to-outcome connection clear to people, and they have confidence that the connection will be the same in the future. Your job as a manager is to be clear on what outcomes should be based on evaluations. Then, make the connections clear, make sure these outcomes are based on valid evaluations, and that your subordinates perceive them as valid.

Do not expect everyone to agree that the reward system is fair. This is almost impossible because we all see the factors that should determine how much outcome we get in different ways. In addition, people don't usually agree on the factors that should be considered in determining outcomes. Some think the only important factor should be performance. Others think factors such as need, seniority, and job knowledge should count. Even if all were to agree on what

Table 8.1. Possible Outcomes

Category	Outcomes
Compensation	Salary or pay rate, bonuses, stock options, fringe benefits
Supervision	Technical knowledge, human relations, fairness
Co-workers	Friendliness, cooperation, commitment to the organization
Security	Job, specific position in organization, degree of job security
Advancement	Promotion, increased responsibilities
Working conditions	Physical (heat, ventilation, comfort), safety (physical, psychological)
Working time	Time off, flexible working hours
Recognition	Formal—manager, organizational; Informal—manager, peers, and subordinates
Authority	Control over others, using my own work strategies, freedom to use my own judgment
Company policies and practices	Fairness, clarity
Opportunities for self-development	Achievement, developing new skills, training opportunities, development outside of work (e.g., exercise, spiritual development)
Consistency with moral values	Not violating my conscience, no conflicts with family needs, opportunity for social service
Activity	Hours expected, convenience of hours expected, not too busy or too slow, amount of variety
Social status	My job in the organization, my job with my family, organization in the community

factors should be considered, they most likely won't agree on how each person "scores" on these factors. They will not likely agree on each other's performance, their amount of job knowledge, etc. So it is rare for all to agree that the reward system is fair. What the manager needs to do is to make it as fair as possible, realizing that for all to agree it is fair is probably impossible.

The fairness of the reward system is a sensitive issue. Subordinates probably will not want to tell you, their manager, that they think you are not being fair.

Nor will they be comfortable saying in a group meeting that they should get more outcomes than a co-worker. Other methods such as a survey could be helpful in getting at true perceptions.

Evaluation-to-Outcome Connection Diagnosis Roadmap

A good way to start assessing the strength of the evaluation-to-outcome connection is by focusing on compensation. Ask your staff how *compensation outcomes* (pay level, pay raises, bonuses, financial incentives, stock options) are related to *formal and informal evaluations*. It may well be that few compensation outcomes are tied to evaluations, or that subordinates do not know which evaluations influence compensation outcomes.

After you map the important compensation outcomes, do the same with the outcome of recognition. Ask if your subordinates think levels of recognition are determined by how well they are performing (how positive the evaluations of their results are). Next ask what happens to the recognition they get if their evaluations go up or go down. You might get some surprising answers.

Accuracy

As you assess, remember that like the other connections, evaluation-to-outcome connections are perceptions that may or may not be accurate. Significant misperceptions of these connections are common. A good example is promotions. In many organizations, it is not at all clear what factors determine promotions. People may have many different ideas about what is important. Some are convinced that what counts is how you dress, which part of the organization you work in, who your boss is, which customers you get assigned to, your technical prowess, or how personable you are at social functions. If these beliefs are inaccurate and the promotion is important, people will put large amounts of energy into actions that have nothing to do with getting the promotion and the actions done are irrelevant to the organization. A person who puts large amounts of effort into irrelevant actions at the expense of valued actions, and does not get the expected outcome, feels frustrated and confused.

The diagnosis summary is shown in Table 8.2.

Table 8.2. Diagnosis Roadmap: Evaluation-to-Outcome

Definition: An evaluation-to-outcome connection is the relationship between the favorableness of an evaluation and the expected amount of outcome. Taken together, evaluation-to-outcome connections define the reward system.		

Considerations: 1. Outcomes can be tangible (salary, office space, health benefits, project funding) or intangible (autonomy, recognition, personal growth).		

Diagnosing the connection: How strong are the evaluation-to-outcome connections?		

What	*How*	*Listen*
Identify the important formal and informal evaluations that are expected to influence rewards.	Clarify your own understanding of how the range of evaluation levels corresponds to important compensation and recognition outcomes. Graph and check your understanding with your boss and/or Human Resources before working with the unit staff.	• The more one expects outcomes to change when evaluations change, the stronger the evaluation-to-outcome connection. • How clear is the reward system? Are your perceptions different from your boss's?
Identify the important compensation outcomes. These might include pay level, pay raises, bonuses, financial incentives, stock options, and health benefits. Identify the important recognition outcomes.	Ask unit members: • For each important compensation outcome, does changing the evaluation lead to a different outcome? • If we show important compensation and recognition outcomes in a graph plotted against evaluation levels, which outcomes change a lot with different evaluations? Which ones stay the same for most evaluations?	• Do your staff members have different perceptions from yours, and from each other? • Is it reasonable to expect that the available rewards will motivate strong performance, or do most rewards focus on minimum performance?

—continued

Table 8.2. Diagnosis Roadmap: Evaluation-to-Outcome (*continued*)

Diagnosing the determinants: Why is a connection particularly weak or strong? What could explain what you are seeing and hearing?		
Number of outcomes	*Consistency across people*	*Consistency over time*
The more outcomes that are tied to evaluations, the stronger the connection.	People who receive the same evaluation should receive the same level of reward. People who receive different evaluations should receive different levels of rewards.	Evaluation levels that previously produced a reward should be expected to produce the same reward again.
List as many outcomes (positive, negative, internal, external, etc.) as you can. See Table 8.1 to get started. Discuss how each is tied to evaluations.	Do unit members perceive this to be true?	Have expectations changed? Is this change perceived as fair? How clearly have the changing expectations been communicated?
Consider the removal of negative outcomes. It is common that the supervisor can remove some negative outcomes based on performance. Examples are unwanted travel, tedious paperwork, or certain aversive work settings.		

Extended Case: Part 5

Friday, April 5
Conference Call

As Jessica listened to Jose and Marius and then to Susan and Dave talk about the feedback measures they had put in place, she smiled. It was a great start. They spent some time talking about what was considered poor, neutral, good, and excellent; which measures were more and less important; and finally how the feedback would be given. These are key features of any good feedback system. Satisfied, she turned the group to the week's national sales figures.

"Our sales rate is up 4% since last month. That's definitely the right direction. We are also about 30 days into our diagnosis. So far, we've looked at actions-to-results and results-to-evaluations. We still need to look at our evaluations-to-outcomes, but this is probably where we are strongest. Our evaluations are built into our commission system in advance. When sales are high (the evaluation) the commission (outcome) always follows. Our typical salesperson's goal is $200,000 in sales per quarter. If people consistently achieve above that level, not only would they receive a higher commission rate (see specifics below) and possibly our incentive trip, but they would be considered to be high performing. Someone who was consistently not making goal by more than 25% would be evaluated for either low performance or territory re-evaluation.

Sales	Commission rate
$0–$50,000	2%
$51,000–$200,000	2.5%
$200,001+	3%

Jessica concluded that there was a direct link between sales dollars and commission dollars. The group agreed, with one distinction. Managers suggested that sales above target should be rewarded at an even higher rate than sales below or at target. Jessica agreed to put together a new payout model for consideration.

Chapter 9

Diagnosing Outcome-to-Need Satisfaction Connections

Understanding Outcome-to-Need Satisfaction Connections

Outcome-to-need satisfaction connections are the relationships between the level of the outcome and the amount of anticipated need satisfaction. They describe how much we expect outcomes to satisfy our needs. The more satisfaction we expect, the stronger our motivation to achieve the outcome. When you assess the strength of the outcome-to-need satisfaction connection, you are trying to find out how well the outcomes available in the work setting satisfy people's needs. In other words, are the rewards in the reward system powerful enough?

Need *satisfaction* can arise from positive outcomes such as getting recognition or from the removal of something negative, such as getting reassigned from a job you dislike. In both cases, the outcomes produce positive feelings of satisfaction. On the other hand, needs that are *not satisfied* produce negative feelings, that is, need *dissatisfaction*. Examples of outcomes that produce the dissatisfaction of needs are being publicly rebuked, having to work with someone you dislike, or being moved to a new unwanted location.

Examples

The expected need satisfaction from different outcomes for different people will, of course, be quite different. The same outcome will also be different in importance for different people. Some examples are shown in Figure 9.1. The two graphs in the top row show the relationship between needs satisfaction and the outcomes of salary and recognition level for Mark. The graph on the left is for salary and shows salary ranging from $45,000 per year to $90,000 per year. The anticipated satisfaction is

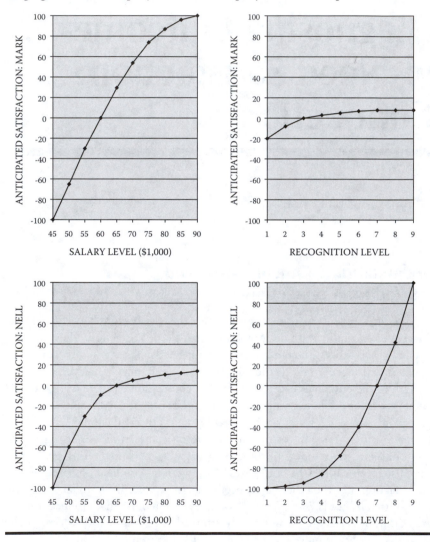

Figure 9.1. Outcome-to-need satisfaction connections: Different outcomes.

on the vertical axis and is depicted by a numeric scale ranging from −100 through 0 to +100. A value of −100 is very negative anticipated satisfaction. A high negative number means Mark will strongly avoid this level of outcome, and if it occurs, it will produce high dissatisfaction. A value of 0 is neutral, that level of the outcome is neither satisfying nor dissatisfying. A value of +100 is extremely attractive.

The graph shows that Mark expects that higher salaries will provide a lot of need satisfaction for him. The function is very steep and goes from very negative to very positive. It also shows that Mark would find a salary of $60,000 neutral in attractiveness. Salary levels above $60,000 would be more and more attractive. Salary levels below that would be more and more negative. Because of this steep connection, salary is a powerful motivator for Mark. In contrast, he is not very motivated by recognition. The graph on the right shows that as recognition increases there would be a small increase in anticipated satisfaction, but not much. Furthermore, the anticipated need satisfaction would hardly change at all once a minimal amount of recognition was given. Clearly, the two outcomes of salary and recognition have very different values for Mark. For him, increased salary levels would be a powerful incentive to improve performance but increased recognition would not.

The graphs on the bottom of the figure are for Nell. They show a very different pattern. For Nell, it is very important for her salary to be at least moderately high. Salary levels below about $60,000 get rapidly more and more negative as shown by the steep drop for lower levels of salary. Note that the shape of the connection graphic for *low* levels of salary is very similar for Nell and Mark. Both would find increases from $45,000 to $60,000 to be very attractive. The difference between them comes at the higher salary levels. For Nell, the increases in anticipated satisfaction for salaries over $70,000 are very small.

However, recognition is very important to Nell, much more important than it is to Mark. Going from low levels of recognition to high levels produces very large increases in anticipated need satisfaction. If she were making $65,000, additional raises would not likely motivate her to change her behavior. When she is making at least $60,000, Nell is much more motivated to improve performance if she expects the outcome will be increased recognition.

Determinants of Outcome-to-Need Satisfaction Connections

Four factors determine the strength of the outcome-to-need satisfaction connection (Figure 9.2). These are (1) the current need state, (2) the number of needs an outcome satisfies, (3) fairness, and (4) expectations and comparisons.

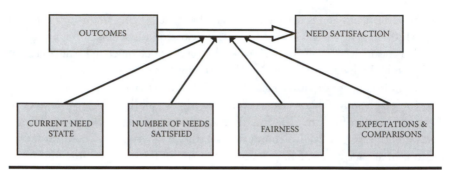

Figure 9.2. Determinants of outcome-to-need satisfaction connections.

Current Need State

As stated earlier, while people have similar needs, we differ greatly in how strong these needs are. Someone with a strong need for affiliation with others will find being alone very unpleasant and will spend considerable effort to be with other people. Someone else with a less strong need for affiliation will like to be with others some of the time, but also be quite content to spend some time alone. The strength of a person's needs is fairly permanent and changes only very slowly over time.

In contrast, the current need state is how much the need is satisfied *at one point in time.* Immediately after eating a meal, our need for food is satisfied. After a few hours, our desire for food starts to increase and continues to increase until we eat again. So our current need state for food changes significantly over a matter of hours. Other needs operate the same way. The current satisfaction of our need for achievement could be very low until we succeed at something that is important. When it occurs, the success satisfies the need for achievement and the current need state decreases. However, over time the need begins to increase and we want more achievement. It takes longer for our need for achievement to start increasing than it does for our need for food, but the basic process is the same.

The current need state is produced by the combination of the strength of that need and how long it has been since that need has been satisfied. The effects of the current need state can be shown in the outcome-to-need satisfaction connection graphs.

Consider the outcome of a promotion, shown graphically in Figure 9.3. The upper left graphic is before the promotion. Because the promotion is an outcome that either is received or is not, the horizontal axis has only two values, No and Yes. The graphic shows that before the promotion, there is a very large difference in the anticipated satisfaction of getting the promotion as compared with not

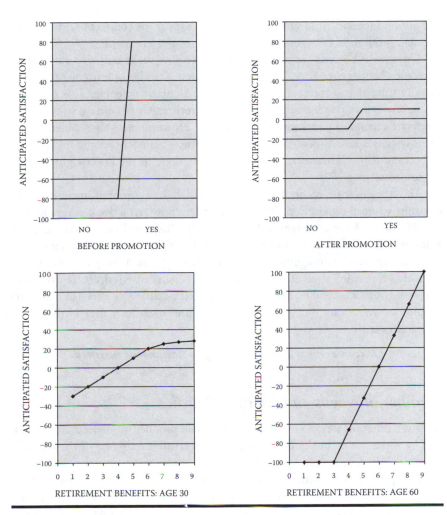

Figure 9.3. Outcome-to-need satisfaction connections: Different times.

getting it. Not getting it leads to −80 in need dissatisfaction; getting the promotion leads to +80.

However, after the promotion is received, the needs associated with that promotion such as recognition, self-esteem, achievement, and being seen as successful are more satisfied. Because of this, the anticipated satisfaction of getting another promotion becomes less. This is shown in the graphic on the right by the much smaller difference in anticipated satisfaction between getting the promotion and not getting it after the first promotion. Just after the promotion has occurred, not getting a *next* promotion has a value of only −10 vs. a value of only +10 for getting it. As time goes on, we would expect to see the value of the next promotion increase. At some point, we would expect the connection graphic for the next promotion to begin to look like that on the left again.

Retirement benefits are another example of how the anticipated value of an outcome changes over time. When we are young, the idea of retirement is so far in the future that it seems unreal and not particularly valuable. This is shown in the lower left graphic where changes in retirement benefits result in only moderate changes in anticipated satisfaction. However, as we get older, retirement becomes much more salient and retirement benefits become much more important. This is shown by the much steeper slope in the lower right graphic for someone at age 60.

The level of current need satisfaction will have a major influence on the outcome-to-need satisfaction connection and on how attractive changes in outcomes will be. A person might feel significantly different about a given outcome a day or a month from now. This also means that a person's needs cannot be permanently satisfied by one outcome. Even if the outcome is very important and it satisfies a person's need at the time, need satisfaction will decrease over time and more outcomes will be needed to keep needs satisfied. Successful managers ensure that important outcomes are available and make sure they are regularly available over time.

Outcomes must occur regularly to keep needs satisfied.

Number of Needs an Outcome Satisfies

If a given outcome satisfies multiple needs, it will produce more need satisfaction and be more powerful than an outcome that satisfies only one of these needs. Consider the example of being assigned a new project. Assume the person sees the new project as a positive outcome and it thus satisfies some needs. Suppose the person is being assigned this new project because she has done a good job in the past and has improved certain skills. If the manager makes it very clear that these are reasons why she is being given the new assignment, the manager is adding outcomes and thus need satisfaction to the outcome of the new assignment. The new assignment now satisfies the additional needs of recognition and a desire for self-improvement.

Another example is when someone has done an especially good job. You could tell that person alone, but if you also know that he values public recognition, you could then tell everyone in the unit and add to the recognition outcome. Now the person not only receives recognition from the boss, but also gets recognition from peers. The point here is to consider how to add satisfaction to an outcome for a person. It is often possible to make outcomes more powerful by making relatively small changes that allow for the satisfaction of more needs.

Fairness

As previously discussed, people are very sensitive to the fairness of organizational reward systems. Good work should be positively rewarded, and poor work negatively rewarded, each commensurate to the value of the contribution made. Outcomes should be applied consistently across people and across time.

If someone believes the organization is not being fair, this decreases the need satisfaction of an outcome. An example would be how outcomes such as raises and promotions are tied to evaluations. If the evaluations are seen as unfair, the positive outcomes that come from the evaluations lose some of their attractiveness. Suppose I believe that the evaluation system is largely random or is based primarily on favoritism. The merit raise I get from this evaluation will not satisfy my needs for recognition and achievement nearly as much as the same raise would if I saw the evaluation system as fair.

Expectations and Comparisons

The last determinant of outcome-to-need satisfaction connections is related to *expectations* and *comparisons* we make about the outcomes we receive. Our expectations heavily influence the need satisfaction we get from outcomes. Someone may get assigned to a new office which is much nicer than the old one. The office may be very attractive to the person and thus the anticipated need satisfaction is high. However, if this person believes he or she should have gotten the office much sooner, the degree of need satisfaction is reduced. Getting the office when the person expected to get it would have produced a higher level of need satisfaction.

We all compare the outcomes we get with what others get. This is human nature. If our outcomes compared with others' outcomes seem equitable, this produces satisfaction. If what we get seems less than equitable, dissatisfaction results.

We certainly expect that the amount of the outcome will have a large effect on the level of need satisfaction. The larger the raise is, the greater the need satisfaction. However, expectations and comparisons with others have a surprisingly large effect as well. Consider the example of a pay raise as shown in the four graphics in Figure 9.4. The upper left graphic shows that, as the size of the pay raise increases, the anticipated need satisfaction also increases.

For this person, let's call him Paul, there is a fairly strong linear relationship between the amount of the outcome (size of the raise) and the anticipated need satisfaction. A pay raise of 6% is the neutral level, indicating that a 6% raise is neither positive nor negative; it is what would be OK. We will call this Paul's baseline outcome-to-need satisfaction connection.

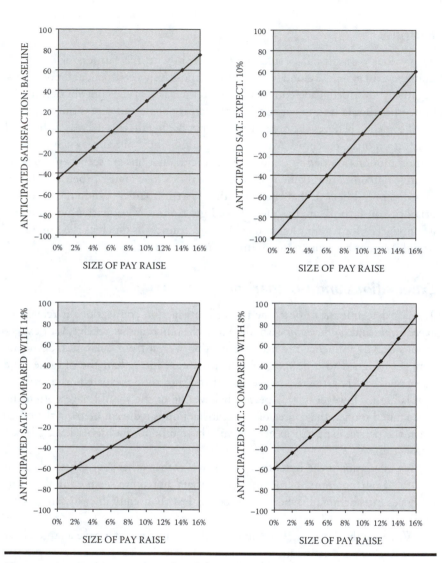

Figure 9.4. Outcome-to-need satisfaction connections: Expectations and comparisons.

However, suppose Paul's boss Elizabeth tells him that she has recommended a 10% raise for him. Paul now changes his expectation to a 10% raise. This changes the outcome-to-need satisfaction connection. This is shown in the upper right graphic. Note that the function is still a straight line, but the entire line is lower. All raise levels now produce lower levels of anticipated satisfaction. Because the expectation has changed to a 10% raise, the same 10% raise now has an anticipated satisfaction level of 0. The 6% raise that Paul originally expected is now quite dissatisfying. It has a satisfaction value of −40. By raising expectations, the anticipated satisfaction of outcomes decreases. If Paul were now to get the 6% raise, he would be dissatisfied, even though before the change in expectations, the 6% would have satisfied him.

The bottom two graphics show the effects of comparisons with others. Suppose that after the conversation with his boss Elizabeth, Paul actually gets the 10% raise. However, he finds out that a co-worker, whose performance is equal to his, received a 14% raise. Because of this comparison, Paul's satisfaction with his 10% raise decreases. The lower left graphic shows that after the comparison, the satisfaction level of the 10% raise is now −20. The comparison has decreased Paul's satisfaction with his raise. Such comparisons can also go the other way. Suppose Paul gets the 10% raise and finds that people he compares with get a raise of 8%. This could increase the satisfaction of the 10% raise. In the lower right graphic, this 10% raise now gets a satisfaction level of about +20.

The amount of need satisfaction is typically one third due to the amount of the outcome, one third the expectation, and one third the comparison with others.

Outcome-to-Need Satisfaction Diagnosis Roadmap

When we try to determine how well outcomes satisfy needs, we sometimes think about the importance of outcomes in a way that is too simple. We ask, for example, how important benefits are or whether recognition is more important than interesting work. These are difficult questions for people to answer and don't provide the information the manager needs to make improvements in motivation in order to improve performance.

Consider again the examples in Figure 9.1. If we ask Nell whether salary or recognition is more important, it will be difficult for her to answer. The overall slope of the graph for recognition is steeper than it is for the salary graph. Thus, one could say she values recognition more than salary. But this is not always the case. If her salary is low, increases in salary are very important and just as important as increases in recognition. However, if her salary is moderate, increases in recognition are much more important than increases in salary.

What this means for the diagnosis is that the question is not how valuable salary or recognition is. What is important is the connection, the *relationship* between outcome level and satisfaction level. So a better question is how valuable *increases* in salary or *increases* in recognition are. If increases (or decreases) are not important, then changes in that outcome will not motivate.

Of all the connections, diagnosing outcomes-to-needs satisfaction is the most sensitive and requires the most care. Most people do not think much about their needs and how well their work outcomes satisfy them. Some people may feel that the value they place on outcomes is private and not anyone else's business. Also, there are likely to be significant differences among individuals in how outcomes satisfy needs. All these factors make it challenging to discuss need satisfaction.

Therefore, an effective approach is to focus the conversation on outcomes and not on needs. Individuals can indicate a relative value for increases or decreases in each outcome or can actually try to draw the connection graphics themselves. This can be done without having to discuss why they feel this way, that is, the more personal issues of which needs are being satisfied. Focus instead on what would increase or decrease satisfaction based on the outcomes available or on outcomes that are not currently available but desired. Private follow-up conversations could be held to discuss any insights that the exercise produces.

Accuracy

Each of us has had a lifetime's experience estimating how attractive different outcomes are to us. We feel confident in anticipating how attractive future outcomes will be to us. However, it is also possible to be wrong, especially when we have not had that outcome previously. We think we want the promotion, but when we get it, the added pressure and responsibility turn out to be more unpleasant than we expected. Are you or your subordinates being realistic about the need satisfaction that an outcome will bring?

Are your expectations of how well an outcome
will meet your needs accurate?
It is rare for a middle-aged man to buy a second red Corvette.

Importance of Other Reward Systems

When diagnosing, consider that there will always be more reward systems operating than you can observe. The work setting can provide outcomes for many of a person's needs. However, work cannot provide outcomes for *all* needs. Family, friends, social and religious groups, and personal development all provide important outcomes that meet important needs. People will (and should!) devote time and effort to meeting needs outside of the organization. In turn, these external reward systems influence behavior at work. The principles are exactly the same. In fact, one can use the motivation model to diagnose motivation in any setting including your own motivation for tasks at home or the motivation of your children at school.

It is not a manager's job to make work satisfy all needs, but to realize that an inherent conflict between need satisfaction in the workplace versus non-workplace exists and can often explain behavior that doesn't make sense when looking only at work.

The diagnosis summary is shown in Table 9.1.

Extended Case: Part 6

Monday, April 5

Jessica had wondered all along about how she would address the outcomes-to-need satisfaction connection. With her new appreciation of the complexities of motivation, Jessica thought there was something more than commission that motivated her sales force. Obviously commissions were very important, but maybe not enough to encourage people to push through the harder times. She had spent the week meeting with small groups of salespeople for breakfast. What was it they loved? Why did they do this job? What made them feel proud? She tried to identify outcomes other than money that would satisfy their needs.

Armed with this information, she suggested that her managers develop some special recognitions and take more care with telling the success stories of individuals who tried new things (both would be new outcomes). The group discussed whether trips to Bermuda were really the best motivator (outcome) for their high performers. Maybe this outcome would not satisfy everyone's needs.

Table 9.1. Diagnosis Roadmap: Outcome-to-Need Satisfaction

Definition: The outcome-to-need satisfaction connection is the perceived relationship between level of the outcome and anticipated need satisfaction. It describes how much we expect an outcome to satisfy our needs.

Considerations:
1. The more we expect the outcome to satisfy our needs, the greater is its attraction.
2. Need satisfaction is very personal and varies greatly among people.
3. We are not always aware of what our needs are, and what things will satisfy them.
4. Efforts to satisfy needs away from work will also influence behavior at work.

Diagnosing the connection: How strong are the outcome-to-need satisfaction connections?

What	How	Listen
Think of some broad categories of outcomes such as: • Control over my work • Time spent at work • Recognition • Compensation	For each class of outcome, how satisfying would it be to get more of that outcome or to get less of it? Do this exercise for yourself and then with unit members. How important is each of these outcomes compared with each other? Is control twice as important as compensation?	• What seem to be the most important satisfiers? • What do you learn about which rewards are valuable to which individuals? • What would need to improve in order to increase satisfaction? Is there one thing that could make the most difference? • Is the anticipated satisfaction realistic?

—continued

Diagnosing the determinants: Why is a connection particularly weak or strong? What could explain what you are seeing and hearing?			
Current need state	*Number of needs satisfied*	*Fairness*	*Expectations and comparisons*
While current need state is an important determinant, you do not need to address it directly. Diagnosing the anticipated satisfaction of outcomes will automatically include current need state.	List important available outcomes. How can outcomes be changed to be more satisfying? This will often mean tying them more closely to a fair assessment of performance. When congratulations, new assignments, compensation increases, and promotions are given, are they communicated in a way that meets multiple needs?	Are there ways in which satisfaction from receiving a reward is lost because the reward does not seem … • Of fair value to the contribution made? • Fair to others? • Fair over time?	Is the expected outcome different from what is delivered? Do comparisons with others increase or decrease satisfaction? Are expectations and comparisons based on accurate information?

IMPROVING MOTIVATION

Chapter 10

Making Improvements

Based on your diagnosis, you've decided that you need to make some changes to improve motivation in your workplace. What changes will you make? What will happen when you make the changes? This chapter examines how to make the needed changes for each component of the model.

As we examine each connection, keep in mind that before the repair of a single component will have a positive effect on motivation, the rest of the connections must be good. For example, suppose your diagnosis indicates that there is a problem with the action-to-results connection. If you fix that problem, things should improve, but only if there are no major problems in the other connections. All the connections must be in good condition for motivation to be good.

Consider every component in the motivation process
when making changes to a single component.

Action-to-Results Connection Improvements

Recall that the first step in the diagnosis of the action-to-results connections was to check the amount of control people believe they have in producing their results. If there were problems with this connection, the next step was to diagnose the determinants. Table 10.1 summarizes the determinants for action-to-results connections and lists the possible problems that might need attention. These were discussed in chapter 6 and are shown in the left-hand column. The right-hand column identifies examples of what can be done to improve the connection.

Table 10.1. Optimizing Action-to-Results Connections

Problem	Solution
Capability	
1. Lack of general ability to do all the actions required to produce the results.	Selection, reassignment
2. Lack of job-specific knowledge and skill to do all the actions required to produce the results.	Training: either formal or on the job, reassignment
3. Person does not believe he or she has the ability and knowledge/skill to produce the results.	Training, experience, encouragement, good feedback
Resources	
4. Lack of resources to do the actions: materials, information, lack of other constraints, etc.	Manager and subordinates ensure resources are available
Authority	
5. Insufficient authority or control to do the needed actions.	Manager provides more autonomy
Work strategies	
6. People must know how to combine actions to generate the desired results, i.e., have a good work strategy.	Training, experience, providing advice from the manager or peers with good strategies
7. In some settings, there must be reasonable agreement among subordinates and between subordinates and the manager on optimal work strategies.	Training, experience, providing advice from the manager or peers with good strategies
8. People must be given the opportunity to develop and test new work strategies.	Manager provides the opportunity, makes sure there is a good feedback system

Capability

The first determinant is capability. A person's action-to-results connections may be low because of permanent, general ability (1). The person does not have the ability to do the actions that will produce the desired results. Without the ability, improvement efforts such as training will have little effect. One long-term solution is better selection. Try to ensure that in the future, people selected for that job do have the capability. For the immediate problem, consider reassigning that person to tasks he or she can do.

If the problem is lack of job-specific knowledge and skill (2), the problem is easier to deal with. Here, the focus should be on training. This can include providing instruction with assignments by the supervisor, on-the-job coaching by successful peers, formal training programs, or self-study, to name a few. This person could also be reassigned to other tasks.

However, remember that there is a difference between actual and perceived capabilities. People may have low action-to-results connections because they do not *believe* they have the capability to do the needed actions (3). The manager must make a judgment here. If the person in fact does not have the capability, it is problem 1 or 2. If the person actually does have the capability, what is needed is more experience combined with encouragement to do the actions and assurance that he or she can do them. With successful experience and positive feedback on that task the person will begin to see he or she actually does have the ability.

Resources

If lack of resources (4) is the problem, the manager must work with subordinates and get very clear about what resources are needed. These resources could include time, staff, supplies, tools, or information. Once these are identified, the manager and subordinates work together to make sure these resources are available. This sometimes means setting up new work procedures within the group. It can also mean working with other units outside the manager's direct control to get the resources when they are needed.

Authority

The problem can be that the subordinates do not have the authority to do the needed actions (5). This becomes a judgment call for the manager. If you can, and feel it is appropriate, give them the needed authority. In some cases, the manager will need to get additional authority as well.

Work Strategies

The next determinant is work strategies. If you feel one or more people in your unit are not using good strategies to do the work (6), a number of solutions are possible. If the problem is with an isolated person or two, good options are discussing better strategies with them and having them coached by someone who uses a better strategy. If many of your subordinates have poor work strategies, a better solution may be to discuss strategies as a group. In such a meeting, have experienced people with good strategies share their effective practices. In some work settings, it is important that everyone uses the same work strategy (7), whereas in other settings different people using different strategies is not a problem. If everyone needs to use the same strategy, use the same solutions as for 6—coaching or group discussions.

It is also critical that subordinates be given the opportunity to develop and test new work strategies (8). This is the way to continually improve strategies and thus continually improve action-to-results connections. The manager is responsible for providing this opportunity. This typically means face-to-face meetings held on a regular basis where the subordinates and the manager can discuss work strategies. In such meetings, ideas for better ways of doing the job can be suggested and discussed. Both the manager and the subordinates must be able to *evaluate* whether the new strategies improve things. This information enables the individual or group to develop better strategies. More considerations about feedback systems are provided later in this chapter.

Results-to-Evaluation Connection Improvements

The possible problems and example solutions for results-to-evaluation connections are summarized in Table 10.2.

Knowing Valued Results

If your diagnosis indicates that subordinates are not clear on what are the important results (1), the solution is to discuss this with them. Review a prioritized list of major results together. If there is disagreement in what you each see as important, explain *why* you each think some results are more important than others. You may be surprised and revise some of your own ideas on importance. In any event, these discussions should result in better agreement on what are the more important and less important results.

Consistency With Broader Organization

The first part of consistency is whether results are consistent with the objectives of the broader organization (2). Ask yourself: If your unit did a good job on the result, exactly as it is measured, how would the organization benefit? Talk this over with subordinates so they can understand your reasoning, especially if this analysis results in changes in measures or priorities.

Table 10.2. Optimizing Results-to-Evaluation Connections

Problem	Solution
Knowing valued results	
1. It is not clear what the valued results are.	Hold discussions between the manager and subordinates.
Consistency with broader organization	
2. Results considered important are not consistent with the objectives of the broader organization.	Careful attention by manager and subordinates to ensure results have a clear line of sight to broader organizational objectives.
3. How results are evaluated is not consistent with actual value of results to the organization.	Careful analysis by manager and subordinates to ensure evaluations match value to the organization.
Agreement among evaluators	
4. People are not clear on the evaluations made by all relevant evaluators.	Discussion with subordinates on who relevant evaluators are and how these evaluations are made.
5. All important evaluators do not agree on the results-to-evaluation connections.	Discussion between manager and subordinates, including consultation with higher management and other evaluators.

The other aspect of consistency with the broader organization is matching the evaluation system to what is valuable to the organization (3). If your diagnosis indicates a mismatch here, it will usually be between what your subordinates see as *your* evaluation and what is valuable to the organization. Discussion with them can clarify misperceptions, but it is sometimes difficult to get subordinates to talk if they think it means criticizing you and facing possible negative consequences from you.

Reassure them that you want to know and try not to become defensive. Such a discussion must be followed by making sure your evaluations in the future are consistent with value to the organization. If you yourself have concerns about the organization's values, your options are trying to change the organization's values, leaving the organization, or living with the mismatch.

Agreement Among Evaluators

If subordinates are not clear on who the relevant evaluators are (4), this is usually a fairly easy fix. Lack of clarity about evaluators comes about most often when individuals don't see the connection between their work and their internal or external customers. Discussion with subordinates about who these evaluators are and why their evaluations are important will usually clear this up.

Getting agreement among evaluators (5) on the results-to-evaluation connections can be difficult. Different evaluators are going to value different things. In your diagnosis, one step was to identify the important evaluators. Clearly, you as the manager are an important evaluator and each person in your unit is an important evaluator. If the mismatch occurs here, the discussions we have been describing above are the way to resolve it. If the mismatch is with customers of your unit, you or members of the unit can meet with the internal or external customers and to clarify where these differences are. This will lead to discussions to try to better align these evaluation systems. Sometimes, having these discussions is all that is needed. In other cases, there is no reconciliation possible. If this is the case, openly acknowledging differences in priorities will be better than not dealing with them at all.

Remember that getting perfect agreement among the evaluators, especially evaluators outside the organization, will not be possible. This is especially true for your and your subordinates' own families. What your family wants from you is probably going to be quite different from what the organization wants. The goal is not to make them identical, but to reconcile them enough to be successful with both.

As you attempt to get the results-to-evaluation connections of different evaluators into alignment, your conversation could include what results are relevant and their relative importance, what level of output is expected in each result, and how different levels of results translate into evaluations.

The Feedback System

The last determinant of results-to-evaluation connections is the quality of the feedback system. We explained the characteristics of a good feedback system in chapter 7 and they were summarized in Table 7.2. Good feedback systems are challenging to create, but incredibly important. If your feedback system seems to be the problem, it is worth the effort to try to fix it. Improving the feedback system in most workplaces will lead to significant improvements in motivation and performance.

We will go through each necessary feature of feedback and discuss how to fix it.

Group versus individual. If the work is done interdependently, base the measures and feedback on group output, not individual output. In a few cases where people work largely independently, such as some sales or maintenance jobs, individual measures can be used. However, these jobs are rare and in many cases the person must still coordinate with others to get the work done right. It is also possible to have both individual- and group-level measures in the feedback system. Be sure to talk with your subordinates to obtain their input before making final decisions on this.

If group-level feedback is to be used, the size of the group is an issue. The size will be determined by how many people work together to accomplish the same objectives. This will normally be groups of 5 to 50 people.

Based on quantitative results and all results. The feedback system needs to be based on the actual results, that is, the output of the unit. It should also be based primarily on quantitative information, and it should measure all important results. This means it must be tied directly to the results/outputs you are trying to produce. Developing good measures of these results is a very difficult task. What most organizations do is use the measures that are readily available or easy to collect. This almost always produces a feedback system that does not cover all the important results. Quantity is measured, but not quality. Speed is measured but not how well the customers' needs are met. So, go through each of the important results and do an analysis of whether that result is being measured well. Remember that most results will require more than one measure.

> **Measuring only some of the important results sends the**
> **message that those not measured are not important.**

Start with the three to eight major results that were identified in the diagnosis. Think of these as objectives for the unit. Then come up with 8 to 15 measures of these results/objectives. In our experience, it is fairly easy to come up with the major results, but it takes about 15 to 25 hours of discussion with your subordinates to come up with really good measures for all of the results.

Control over measures. As part of this analysis, make sure that the measures used are ones your subordinates have control over. Frequently, the easily available measures are not ones that the people doing the work can control. This is deadly to action-to-results connections. So go through each measure with the people in your unit, and focus on controllability. This will almost always mean changing some of the measures. It will usually not be possible to have all measures completely under subordinates' control, but try to develop measures that maximize this control as much as possible.

Everyone understands the system, relative importance is captured, and feedback is valid. Understanding the feedback system means everyone knows what the important results are, they know and understand how each measure is derived, they know the relative importance of the different measures, and they know how the feedback information will be used. In evaluating your feedback system, go through each of the measures carefully. Make sure you *and your subordinates* know exactly where the data are coming from and how the measure is calculated. It is common to get some surprises when you actually check this. Often, measures you use turn out to be derived in a different way than you thought. This is also a good time to discuss the relative importance of the different measures. Such discussions will help not only with the validity and perceived validity of the system, but also with understanding the system.

Appropriate level of specificity. In going through each measure, also assess whether it is at the appropriate level of specificity. You do not want either too much or too little detail. This must be done in consultation with your subordinates. They will know what level of detail they need. The goal is to get the specificity at a level that will allow them to identify where they need to change their work strategies to make improvements.

Descriptive and evaluative information. Your feedback system must not only include descriptive measures of results but also evaluative measures. This is the how much versus how good issue. Knowing 90% of customer orders were completed on time is a descriptive measure. Knowing that 90% is unacceptably low is an evaluative measure. There are a number of ways to include this evaluative information in the feedback system. Some techniques are fairly simple; some are more complex.

Feedback must include how much and how good.

Probably the easiest system is to identify ranges on the measure that correspond to levels of evaluation. For example, in the percent of customer orders on time, start with what is the minimum acceptable range. This minimum acceptable range is the amount of the result that is neither especially good nor especially bad. It is the level that meets expectations but does not exceed them. Suppose after discussion with subordinates, you and your unit decide this acceptable range is from 98% to 98.5% orders on time.

Next, define what is a good range versus what is an excellent range. The good range might be 98.6% to 98.9% while the excellent range is 99% to 100%. Then do the same for the range that is considered low (e.g., 95% to 97.9%) and the range that is considered unacceptable (below 95%). You should define these ranges for each measure.

If these ranges are developed and communicated to unit personnel, everyone knows what level of the result gets translated into what level of the evaluation. However, it is essential that the ranges be determined by discussion with your subordinates to gain their input and involvement. They will often be able to add valuable information in developing these ranges. This will help greatly in clarifying results-to-evaluation connections.

Acceptance and fairness. Analysis of the feedback system will usually mean measures need to be added or changed, so plan to spend considerable time on this. It is a complex issue and takes a lot of thinking. Subordinates should be involved in all of these discussions. If you have too many subordinates, meet with a subset and develop a process of getting the inputs from *all* subordinates as this analysis process goes on. This can be through meeting notes or periodic meetings with all subordinates to summarize progress. Another approach that works well is to have some subordinates who are permanent members of this discussion group and have the remaining subordinates rotate through the discussion group for different meetings. This heavy involvement at all steps of the process is important because subordinates will be an excellent source of information on what the good measures are and how much control they have over the measures. This participation in the design of the feedback system is by far the *best* way to gain acceptance of the system and for subordinates to see firsthand that the system is valid and fair.

Timely feedback. As part of the analysis, make sure you can get the information needed for feedback as soon as possible after the work is done. Feedback given for work completed months ago is not nearly as effective as feedback on more recent work. This will be easier for some measures than for others, but try to come up with measures and ways of collecting these measures that minimize the lag time.

Regular schedule. As part of the feedback redesign, plan to have the measurement and evaluation data put together into a formal feedback report which is then given to your subordinates on a regular, predictable time interval. The interval you use will depend on the nature of the work you are doing. If one unit of work is finished in a matter of a few days or less, feedback once a week is appropriate. If it takes a week or two to complete one unit of work, monthly feedback is usually best. In some cases where a unit of work takes months, longer intervals are usually appropriate. What is important is to decide with your subordinates on a specific interval that everyone agrees will be most helpful. Then be sure to follow that schedule.

Use feedback for improvements. After each feedback report, plan to have a meeting with the entire unit to review the report. This review is to let unit personnel know how well they have been doing over the last time interval. Having what they believe is valid information on how much they have done and how valued their performance is will solidify the results-to-evaluation connections very effectively. Devote the bulk of the feedback meeting to a discussion of how to improve performance. The idea is to use the feedback information to develop new strategies for doing the work. For example, a developing problem may be due to not getting the needed information from another unit on time. The group may decide that one person needs to be in better contact with that other group in order to get the information sooner.

Focus the discussion on what can be done to improve things. As new strategies are tried, use subsequent feedback to see if the new approach worked by looking for improvements in the measures. If the new approach is working, keep using it or try to improve it even further. If the measurement data indicate that the new strategy is not working, try a new approach.

It is very easy to create a bad feedback system.

Stability. Once the feedback system is in place, it is important that it remains stable. For good results-to-evaluation connections to form, people must see how the results and the evaluation relate over a period of time. If the feedback system is changed too often, it is much more difficult to form clear results-to-evaluation connections. However, the system *does* need to be changed when the unit's mission changes or there is a change in technology. If these changes influence the feedback system, definitely make the changes, but be sure that everyone knows how the system will be changed and why it is being changed.

Thus, good feedback is critical for motivation. Not only does it improve results-to-evaluation connections, but it makes it much easier to develop good work strategies (action-to-results connections), as well as adding powerful outcomes such as recognition, achievement, and a feeling of being empowered (outcome-to-need satisfaction connections), all of which are necessary for high performance (evaluation-to-outcome connections).

Evaluation-to-Outcome Connection Improvements

Next are the evaluation-to-outcome connections. Possible problem areas and examples of solutions are shown in Table 10-3.

Number of Outcomes

The first possibility is not having enough outcomes tied to evaluations (1). Most managers first think of adding incentives when they think of improving motivation—incentives intended to create higher motivation and performance. Formal incentives have several pitfalls such as motivating only the measured behavior, possibly undermining team effectiveness if rewards are individual based, or undermining individual motivation if the rewards are team based; they can also be expensive, and they must often be increased over time in order for them to feel like something extra.

In trying to identify other outcomes to tie to evaluations, remember that there are many types of outcomes beyond tangible incentives. Some outcomes are internal, such as a feeling of accomplishment. Refer to Table 8.1 for ideas. By using the example of an accomplishment, an evaluation-to-outcome connection could be enhanced by describing what was evaluated and why this was

Table 10.3. Optimizing Evaluation-to-Outcome Connections

Problem	*Solution*
Number of outcomes	
1. Not enough outcomes are tied to evaluations.	Consider a wider range of outcomes, increase ties between existing outcomes and evaluations, and try to remove negative outcomes.
2. The consequences of good and poor performance are not clear.	Communicate clearly to personnel what the connections are. Do not assume they are known.
Consistency across people	
3. Different people get different outcomes for the same performance.	Identify whether problems are actual or perceived. If perceived, explain why different people get different outcomes. If actual, be more consistent.
Consistency across time	
4. The consequences of good and poor performance are not consistent across time.	Identify whether problems are actual or perceived. If perceived, explain why different people get different outcomes. If actual, explain why things have changed.

an accomplishment. An alternative to adding a positive outcome is removing a negative outcome based on performance. In discussing outcomes with your subordinates, try to identify things they don't like that you can remove if performance is high. Examples would be not having to write certain types of reports or providing more discretion in decision making if performance is high.

Consequences of Good and Poor Performance

If people do not know the consequences of good and poor performance (2), this means they do not have accurate evaluation-to-outcome connections. In one sense, this is an easy problem to fix. Sit down with your subordinates and discuss what they see as consequences, then talk about what you see as consequences. There may be many more consequences than they realized. In preparing for such a discussion, give some thought to what you use as consequences of your evaluations. The difficult situation is when the consequences for good and poor performance are largely the same. Then you are back to dealing with the more difficult issue discussed in (1), finding more powerful outcomes.

Consistency Across People and Time

Both consistency across people (3) and consistency across time (4) are aspects of fairness. If your reward system is seen as unfair, it reduces the evaluation-to-outcome connections because people cannot correctly anticipate what outcomes will occur following high or low performance.

Let's start with consistency across people. Clarify whether the problem is a *perceived* lack of consistency or a *real* lack of consistency. If the problem is due to incorrect perceptions, it can often be corrected by adding information. It may be that some subordinates do not know why someone received an outcome such as a special assignment or a better office. If these are attractive outcomes to them and they feel their work is just as good, they are going to believe the reward system is unfair. If there was a good reason for providing these outcomes, explain what that reason was. If you don't see their performance as being as good as the person who received the outcome, tell them and tell them why. While this is usually an unpleasant task, the negative feedback will have positive effects on the evaluation-to-outcome connections if it serves to help them to perceive the evaluation as fair.

If different people actually do receive different outcomes for the same performance, this is going to reduce evaluation-to-outcome connections and thereby reduce motivation. The first step is to acknowledge that there is a problem and that you want to fix it. Then work with subordinates and your own management to try to make the reward system more consistent. However, don't assume you can find a solution that will make everyone happy. It usually cannot be done. There will almost always be some residual feelings that the system is unfair. The best you can hope for is to keep these feelings to a minimum.

> *It is impossible to create a reward system*
> *that everyone thinks is fair.*

For consistency across time, the needed improvements are essentially the same. First, try to determine whether the problem is real or a result of misperceptions. If it is due to misperceptions, explain why what seems to be an inconsistency is actually not. If the problem is real, explain why the change was made. If there is not a good reason, work on the reward system to make it more consistent over time. In the future, if a change needs to be made, be very clear to your subordinates what the change will be, why it is being made, and how it affects their own reward system.

Outcome-to-Need Satisfaction Connection Improvements

The last connection is the outcome-to-need satisfaction connection. Table 10.4 shows possible problems and example solutions.

Current Need State

The first possibility is that the available outcomes are not valuable to the person (1). In your analysis and action plan, it is important to distinguish outcomes that are tied to evaluations of performance from those that are not. If there are not enough important outcomes tied to evaluations, there is little motivation for high performance. Outcomes not tied to performance also produce need satis-

Table 10.4. Optimizing Outcome-to-Need Satisfaction Connections

Problem	*Solution*
Current need state	
1. Available outcomes are not valuable to the person.	Try to identify other outcomes, remember current need state may differ over time and needs must be regularly satisfied.
Number of needs satisfied	
2. Outcomes are not tied to as many needs as possible.	Evaluate major outcomes to see if they can be tied to other outcomes, pay particular attention to outcomes that could be tied to achievement and recognition.
Fairness of the reward system	
3. Outcomes of good and poor performance are not perceived as consistent across recipients and over time (i.e., fairness).	Maximize consistency as much as possible, explain when apparent inconsistency occurs.
Expectations and comparisons	
4. Expectations of getting outcomes are not realistic.	Be very careful about raising expectations; discuss expectations when they seem unrealistic.
5. Personnel use inappropriate comparisons.	Ask about whom subordinates compare with, explain why differences exist.

faction even though they do not add to motivation to perform *well*. Such outcomes make it valuable for the person to continue working for the organization. So, if keeping good people in your organization is an issue, look at outcomes that are tied to performance *and* outcomes that are not. Pay special attention to negative outcomes people believe happen to them such as lack of recognition, not being treated with respect, and having no clear career development path.

In either case, the manager and unit team members must try to identify other valuable outcomes. Great managers take an interest in learning what outcomes are most satisfying to different individuals. A manager holding a sales promotion may tell one staff member to make 10 telephone calls and then he can go home, while telling another, "Let's see how many calls you can complete in an hour." In one case, the outcome emphasis is on minimizing time at work; in the other case, it is on maximizing achievement. The work assignment is roughly identical, but the manager knows her staff well enough to provide equivalent but different outcomes.

Keep in mind that the need-satisfying power of outcomes varies greatly from person to person and for the same person over time. The current need state changes over time so that a need that was satisfied at one point in time will become unsatisfied over time and require more outcomes. Thus, outcomes must be provided on a regular basis to keep needs satisfied.

Number of Needs Satisfied

We have talked about attaching outcomes to as many needs as possible (2). In diagnosis, you looked at the major outcomes to see if the satisfaction of other needs might be feasible. This will be the easiest for outcomes related to recognition and achievement. For example, when someone, a subgroup, or the whole unit does an especially good job, make sure they know it, and if appropriate, that others know it too. When someone gets an infrequent major outcome such as a promotion, a special award, or special recognition from customers, making that public is also a way to tie the outcome to more recognition and achievement needs.

Fairness of the Reward System

We talked about fairness of the reward system (3) in the section on evaluation-to-outcome connections, but it is relevant here too. In addition to reducing evaluation-to-outcome connections, a reward system that is seen as unfair lowers outcome-to-need satisfaction connections. Receiving a raise based on performance satisfies needs related to money. However, if the reward system is seen as being fair, that same raise will *also* satisfy needs for achievement and recognition.

If the system is fair, the raise accurately indicates that the person did a good job. If the reward system is not fair, getting that raise will not satisfy these additional needs. So a fair reward system helps tie additional needs to the same outcomes. The ways to ensure fairness were discussed above and the same techniques described to maximize fairness could be used here.

Expectations

As a manager, consider that the same level of outcomes could be made more satisfying by having more realistic (i.e., lower) expectations or by having better information when subordinates make comparisons. If your diagnosis indicates that people have unrealistic expectations of outcomes (4), this is something that can be discussed with them. Telling people their expectations of raises, promotions, or other outcomes are unrealistically high is not a pleasant thing to do. However, in the long run it is worth the effort because these unrealistic expectations will lead to disappointments and can substantially reduce the satisfaction when the outcome is actually received.

Managers should also be very careful about raising expectations. To tell people you expect they will get a large raise or be promoted will increase their expectations. Even if they do get the outcome, there will be less satisfaction than if they had not been given the expectation. If they do not get the outcome, this will result in much higher *dissatisfaction* than would have occurred without the expectation being raised.

This is not to say you should *never* tell people that you believe a positive outcome such as a large raise, a promotion, or an award is coming. There are clearly situations where this is appropriate. However, bear in mind that there is a downside to raising expectations and weigh that into the decision to tell people.

Comparison

The last determinant of outcome-to-need satisfaction connections is comparison. If your diagnosis indicates people are using inappropriate comparisons (5), this needs to be addressed. What happens most frequently is that people compare with others that they believe are getting more outcomes for the same level of performance, or are getting the same outcomes for lower levels of performance. The outcomes could be higher pay, lower workload, better working conditions, and so forth. The reaction is: "My work is just as good as theirs, why don't I get what they get?"

As with the other perception determinants, the first step is to see how accurate their perceptions are. If they are right, it is an example of an unfair reward system and it should be addressed using the same techniques for improving fairness discussed above. Often, however, the problem is that the comparison is not an appropriate one. It could be the performance of the person or people they compare with is actually higher and this accounts for the difference in outcomes.

Another possibility is that while other people do get more positive outcomes, they also get more negative ones. For example, they get higher salaries because of the higher cost of living in another city or because they have to travel more. You may not be able to completely satisfy someone with inaccurate perceptions, but explaining the rationale for differences can help reduce perceived unfairness.

As a final point, good reward systems are a large investment by the organization. What should be clear by now is that organizations lose a great deal of the value of these systems if fairness, expectations, and comparisons are not managed well. In many cases, it is far more cost-effective for the organization to put resources into improving these factors, especially fairness, rather than spending more to increase the level of outcomes.

> *It is often more cost-effective to improve the fairness of the reward system than to add costly outcomes.*

Extended Case: Conclusion

Wednesday, April 10, 9 a.m.
Coffee With Pat

"So thirty days in, what's your diagnosis?" Pat asked Jessica.

"Well," said Jessica, "I thought you'd ask, so here's a summary" (Table 10.5).

"Way to go, Jessica. It sounds like you're making some great changes."

"Yes," she said, "Let's hope so. It feels good to have some concrete improvements to announce at the National Sales Conference."

Table 10.5. Summary of the Diagnosis

	Actions-to-results	*Results-to-evaluations*	*Evaluations-to-outcome*	*Outcomes-to-needs satisfaction*
Issue	Inconsistent work strategy	Clarify important results Resolve conflicts among evaluators Feedback system	Strong connection for money	Identify additional satisfying outcomes beyond commission How effective are trips in motivating top salespeople?
Action	Schedule at least 6 weeks out 10 appointments with high value customers per week	Combined Marketing and Accounting Customer and Product Profitability Analysis by region Feedback measures and regular feedback delivery	Increase by adding additional outcomes for sales above target	More forms of recognition and stories of individual achievements More choice of incentives: domestic trips to resorts (with family or guests) or Bermuda trip
Status	60% of sales force has implemented	Planned	In review	Announce at National Conference

Throughout the Year

Shortly after Jessica and her team added the new trip incentives, a stronger high-end incentive plan and regular feedback to the 6-week scheduling strategy, sales began to increase. After 3 months, they were no longer falling behind on their annual goals. The profitability analysis was even more eye-opening. Marketing and Accounting's 6-week analysis turned into a 6-month project. When they were done, it was clear that by changing the sales force's customer emphasis, far more profitability was possible.

As new priorities came along, Jessica worked to maintain the feedback system and continue her distinctive recognition program even when company priorities changed. She took time to make sure that people understood the many benefits of working for their large organization so that valuable individual motivators weren't overlooked. There was generally a perception among the sales force that their goals were tough, but the evaluations and rewards were fair. Retention of talent and customers was good.

It wasn't surprising to her that Marius and Jose had just been asked to move into other functions in the organization with the hope that they could infuse those groups with the same kind of focus on improvement. With new regional managers, Jessica would begin the diagnosis process again, looking for new ways to improve.

May 10, 8 p.m. One Year Later
One Hour After the Close of the
National Sales Conference

"Wow," said Luke Stiles, division president, "What great energy—20% growth in profitability and 40% growth in sales ... as I said in there earlier, they and you should be so proud."

"Yes," said Jessica. "It's amazing what you can do with a little motivation."

Chapter 11

Predicting the Effects of Changes

In the last chapter we described what changes to make based on your motivational diagnosis. In this final chapter we talk about predicting the effects of interventions designed to change motivation. This chapter is designed for those who want to see a more detailed example of using the motivation model. We will use the example of financial incentives. Financial incentives are commonly used as a way to improve motivation. The question is: How should financial incentives be used to improve motivation?

Implementing Financial Incentives

Suppose you are asked to consider implementing a new reward system of financial incentives to encourage high motivation and thus performance. How would you use the motivation model to design an effective system?

First let's be clear on what we mean by a financial incentive system. A financial incentive system is:

- A *formal* program of *regularly occurring* financial awards that are given in addition to salary.
- The awards are based on performance.
- There are formally communicated, pre-defined rules by which the incentives are given.

- These rules are known to all before the performance period.
- The expectation is that the incentive system will continue to operate over time.

Financial Incentives and Motivation

A financial incentive is an amount of money given to a person for achieving a performance level. Thus, it is an outcome. So an incentive system is going to create a change in outcomes. However, as we have stressed many times, we need to look at all of the components of the model in order to understand what will happen to motivation. So we will look at each connection and explore the possible effects of the incentives.

Financial Incentives and Action-to-Results Connections

For a financial incentive system to be effective, the action-to-results connections must be fairly strong. That is, people must believe they have fairly good control over their results. If this is not the case, the value of the incentive system is substantially weakened. The purpose of the incentive system is to make it more attractive to put in high levels of effort and thus produce more results which, when evaluated, lead to the attractive financial incentives. The less control people have over their results, the less effect any incentive will have.

If the action-to-results connections are low, we need to focus on the determinants of these connections: capability, resources, authority, and work strategies.

Much of the cost of incentives is wasted if any one of
the other connections in the model is low.

Capability

One aspect of capability is whether people can produce the results necessary to get the incentives. If some people in the unit do not have the ability or the training to generate the needed results, they will never get the incentives. Instituting a system where some people will never get the incentive will produce significant levels of dissatisfaction for those who don't receive them and they will see the system as unfair. It will also serve as a demotivator to those who cannot get the incentives, and for these individuals, the system will actually lower their performance.

There are also problems for people who are very high in ability. If it is easy for some people to reach the result or output level where they get the incentive, the system will have little effect on them. If they are already performing at the level which produces the incentive, the financial outcome will not lead them to higher performance. For them, their motivation combined with their high level of ability already leads them to perform at this high level. Adding more value to performing at that same level will not lead them to perform at a higher level; it will only make it more satisfying to perform at the level at which they were already performing. This might help improve satisfaction, but it will not help to improve motivation or performance.

This ability issue influences how the incentive system should be designed. The two basic approaches to designing incentive systems are a goal-based system and a continuous improvement system. We will discuss this issue in detail in a later section on evaluation-to-outcome connections, but in a goal-based system, someone receives the incentive if performance exceeds the specific goal. In a continuous improvement system, the higher the performance, the more money is earned. A goal-based system is a problem with high ability people who are already performing above the level where they obtain the incentives. However, in a continuous improvement incentive system, there is always value in improving performance, so a high ability person will be motivated to perform at higher and higher levels. An analogous argument can be made for people of lower ability. If incentives can be earned at lower levels of performance in a continuous improvement system, the incentive system will improve motivation for these lower ability people as well.

Resources

The less people have the needed resources to produce the results, the lower the action-to-results connections, and the weaker the incentive system becomes. Resources include equipment, staff, supplies, information, raw materials, and anything else it takes to produce the results. Consider the example of a machine-based production setting. If some of the machines are older and break down regularly, this will reduce the action-to-results connection. Getting the incentive then depends on how the machine holds up, which is out of the person's control. The same problem exists for any resource needed to produce the results. If these resources are not readily available, the action-to-results connections are reduced and the incentive system is weakened.

Authority and Work Strategies

The final two determinants of action-to-results connections are having the authority to make needed decisions and good work strategies. These determinants also need to be good for an incentive system to work well. The authority issue is usually fairly straightforward and can be dealt with as described in the last chapter on making improvements.

The work strategies issue is more complex. Work strategies operate like ability. Those with a superior work strategy will be able to produce more results than those with an inferior work strategy. This makes getting the incentives easier for those with good strategies. If a person's good strategy already results in performance above the level needed to get the maximum incentive, the new incentive system will have little effect on that person.

If the work strategy is bad enough to keep the person from earning any incentives, the system will have no effect on performance and a negative effect on satisfaction. As with ability, an incentive system based on continuous improvement will help deal with this problem.

Financial Incentives and the Results-to-Evaluation Connections

The next component in predicting the effects of an incentive system is the results-to-evaluation connections. The determinants of results-to-evaluation connections are knowing what results are valued, consistency with the broader organization, agreement between evaluators, and the feedback system.

An incentive system cannot be effective without a
good measurement and evaluation system.

It is important that these determinants are in good condition for an incentive system to be effective. The issues to address for the first three determinants are really the same as those discussed in the last chapter on making improvements. So, if your diagnosis indicates that these are not in good condition, the incentive system will be weakened.

The Feedback System

Where results-to-evaluation connections become essential is in the feedback system. Remember that the feedback system includes both the measurement system and the evaluation system. Both are critical components in the incentive system. To make this clear, we will go through the factors that make up a good feedback system and see how they help predict the effects of an incentive system. However, we can start with one fundamental point: *a good feedback system is absolutely essential for an incentive system to be effective.*

Individual versus group systems. The first feedback characteristic is whether it is an individual-based or a group-based feedback system. This is a critical design decision for an incentive system as well. An individual feedback system has many strengths. In an individual feedback system, as shown in Figure 11.1, each person receives specific feedback on his or her results and the evaluations that go along with those results. With a good individual feedback system, the results-to-evaluation connections will be very high. An individual feedback system also helps to clarify the action-to-results connections because the person knows how much energy was allocated to his or her actions and the level of results is apparent from the feedback.

In a group-based system, each person receives the results and evaluations for the *whole group*, but not for his or her own results. This is shown graphically in the figure where each person (P1, P2, P3, and P4) produces results that are combined into the group result. The feedback system returns to each person the *group level* results and evaluations. Thus, for each person in the group, the results-to-evaluation connections are clear for the entire group. However, each

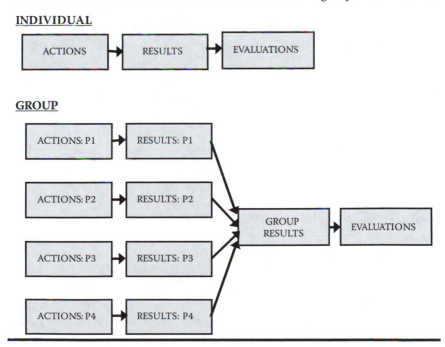

Figure 11.1. Individual versus group feedback.

person's individual contribution to that group result is combined with those of the others in the group. Thus, while the group-level results-to-evaluation connections become very high, the *individual-level* results-to-evaluation connections are not as high because each person is only one source of the combined results. This also serves to lower the individual's action-to-results connections, because now the energy applied to the actions by any given individual is related to the feedback that is the *combined* result of the group's actions.

This means that if the other components of the model are in fairly good condition, an individually based feedback system is going to produce stronger motivation than a group-based system. This sounds like an individually based feedback system must be better than a group-based system and implies that an individual-based *incentive* system will be better than a group-based incentive system. Actually, this is not usually the case. It depends on the type of work being done. If the work is that rare type of work where people work almost completely independently of each other (e.g., insurance sales) an individual-based feedback system is best and an individual-based incentive system is best.

However, for most jobs, people work in a highly interdependent way. In such jobs, it is frequently impossible to accurately measure the unique contributions of each person. We argued in the last chapter that a feedback system for such interdependent work should usually be a group-based system. The same is true of the incentive system.

Although it is true that individual-based feedback and incentive systems are more powerful than group-based systems, a powerful individual-based incentive system will likely produce serious problems in work where people are interdependent. The issue is cooperation. In interdependent work, people have to cooperate with one another in order to get the work done. For example, assume that we have a group of consultants working in the same product area. One important result measure is the number of billable hours. When Rebecca, one of the consultants, is working with a client, sometimes that client needs a service that another consultant could do a better job of providing. With an incentive system tied to her billable hours, Rebecca is much more likely to try to provide that service to her client, even when she knows another consultant in the group could do a better job.

On the other hand, if the incentive is tied to the *group's* billable hours, Rebecca will be much more likely to bring in the other consultant. Thus, for maximum client satisfaction and the long-range success of the consulting firm, it is clearly better to use group-level incentives. Therefore, an individual system creates serious problems when cooperative efforts are necessary in order to do the work. While individual results may go up, the overall results produced by the unit will actually go down. In this situation, the individual incentive system will produce the opposite effect from what was intended.

> *An individual-based incentive system used*
> *on an interdependent work group can be a disaster.*
> *The stronger the incentives, the greater the disaster.*

So, if the work being done requires cooperation between people, as it usually does, a group-based incentive system is best. A group-based incentive system also has other advantages. Because the group output is being used for the incentive, it reduces the problems of differences in ability, resources, and work strategies that we discussed above. For example, if there are differences in the amount of production from different machines, this is not as great a problem if the incentives are awarded on the basis of the entire unit's output. Group-based incentive systems also reduce the problems of people with better strategies having a better chance to earn the incentives. If the incentives are tied to group performance, those with very good or not-so-good strategies are all equally motivated to improve performance. A group-based system also adds motivation for those with better strategies to help others to improve their strategies. If those with suboptimal strategies improve, the entire unit benefits from their higher performance.

However, on the negative side, group incentive systems must deal with the problem of how the incentives are distributed among the members of the group. Differences in experience, skill level, and percentage of time with the group are examples of factors that may lead the group to feel equal distribution of the incentive is not fair. In this case, participation of the group in deciding how to distribute the financial incentive is almost always the best way to resolve or at least to minimize this problem.

Results, feedback, and incentives. Looking at the results that are measured by the existing feedback system also leads to predicting the effects of incentives. Clearly, the measures must be valid and understood, and unit personnel must have control over the results before an incentive system will work well. However, there are some characteristics of results in the feedback system that are especially important.

One such issue is the need to measure *all* the important results. This is one of the areas where many incentive systems fail. If they are based on the measures that are readily available, this usually results in a system that does not include all the important results. For example, the quantity and speed of customer service may be measured but not the quality. If the incentive system is tied to this incomplete set of results, motivation will be increased only for doing the things that are measured. There will be less motivation to do the things that are *not* measured. If the incentive system is powerful, quantity and speed of customer service will go up while quality will go down. The more powerful the incentive system, the more this will happen.

The essential point is that, once again, it is critical that all the important results are measured and included in the incentive system.

Differential importance and overall scores. Another design issue stemming from the criteria for a good feedback system is that you must consider the differential importance of the various results. It is rare to have only one result that is assessed by only one measure. Usually, multiple measures are needed and these measures are going to differ in importance. This means they will differ in how much value they add to the organization. For example, both the level of production and keeping accurate records are important in making furniture, but the level of production is more important.

So, the design issue in an incentive system is how to tie incentives to results/ outputs when, as is usually the case, there are multiple measures that vary in importance. There are really only two ways to do this. One way is to have a certain amount of incentive for differing levels of output on each measure. The amount of the incentive can be made proportional to the level of importance of that measure. To continue with the above example, suppose that each member of the furniture manufacturing unit gets a $100 bonus if production is 10% above target for the week, $200 if it is 15% above target, and $300 if it is 20% above. Each member would also receive a bonus of $25 if 95% of the records are completed accurately and $50 if 100% are completed accurately. So, if production is 10% above target ($200 bonus) and 95% of the records are completed accurately ($25 bonus) the member will receive a total bonus for the week of $225.

This sort of system will work, but is cumbersome to understand and to use. This leads to the second way of dealing with multiple measures: developing a single, overall performance score. If you have such an overall score, it is much easier to tie financial incentives to that one index. However, developing a good single overall index is not easy. There is a series of technical measurement issues involved with generating an overall index which is beyond the scope of this book. If you are interested in this issue, look at Pritchard, Paquin, DeCuir, McCormick, and Bly (2002). If you do not have an overall index you feel comfortable with, it is probably better to build the incentive on multiple measures as above.

Fairness, feedback, and incentives. There are several characteristics needed in a feedback system that relate to fairness and acceptance. The point here is really a relatively simple one. Make sure that your measurement and evaluation systems are actually fair, are perceived as fair, and are accepted by subordinates. Carefully check this *before* installing any incentive system. Also, remember the power of participation in acceptance. If you have subordinates participating heavily in the design of the incentive system, while the system design will take more time, you will increase the acceptance of the system, thereby saving yourself many problems once the system is in place.

If you have an ineffective feedback system, the stronger the financial incentive is, the more damage you will do.

Other needed feedback characteristics. It should be clear that you must have a very good feedback system in place before you start any financial incentive system. We have discussed above the major points that will predict the effects of incentive systems, but it is also valuable to review the other needed feedback system characteristics discussed in the last chapter. Go through all of these criteria and do an honest evaluation of your existing feedback system. If it needs any improvements, make these improvements and use them over time *before* adding an incentive system.

Financial Incentives and Evaluation-to-Outcome Connections

The first determinant of evaluation-to-outcome connections is the number of outcomes. Remember that there are many outcomes, so we first need to identify all the outcomes that are affected by the financial incentive system. Of course, there is the outcome of the money itself, but there are others as well. If the financial outcomes are tied to fairly high levels of performance, which they usually are, getting the outcomes will also provide other outcomes, such as recognition for doing a good job and a feeling of accomplishment. These outcomes are usually intended to occur with an incentive system.

However, unintended outcomes can occur that are not positive. For those who do not get the money, there can be resentment. This will likely be the case for those in the unit who do not get the money, but will also be likely for people in other units who are not part of the incentive system in the first place and, thus, do not have the opportunity to earn the money. Another outcome might be the belief that if people regularly start earning extra money, expectations of performance will increase for everyone and this will add pressure that will be stressful. So in your analysis, you need to consider both the intended and the unintended outcomes.

We also need to ask whether the incentives are needed in the first place. Are there already enough outcomes for performing well? If so, financial incentives are probably unnecessary. In fact, a good feedback system that provides the information for people to get feelings of recognition and achievement provides many of the outcomes the incentive system does. A good feedback system already provides recognition and feelings of achievement for high levels of performance. So if you have a good feedback system, the added positive value of financial outcomes is going to be just the money.

> *A good feedback system is often more effective
> than an incentive system.*

So first consider what positive outcomes are already tied to performance. If there are few such positive outcomes, financial outcomes from the incentive system could provide these needed outcomes. However, if there are already substantial outcomes, incentives may not be necessary.

We also need to consider what will be associated with the financial outcomes, that is, how the evaluation-to-outcome connections will change with the new incentive system? It may seem that incentives will be tied to results, that is, outputs. In a sense this is true, but it is really more accurate to say that incentives will be tied to evaluations. Management will make the decision of what level of results is necessary to get the financial outcome. That is another way of saying that if results are good enough, the incentive will be awarded. As soon as we start talking about what are considered good or not-so-good levels of output (results), we are talking about evaluations. Thus, as the model indicates, the outcomes will be (technically speaking) tied to *evaluations*.

Goal or Continuous Improvement Design?

But how will the tie with evaluations be made? There are many ways to attach the financial incentives to the evaluations. One of the major decisions in designing an incentive system is whether to use a goal system or a continuous improvement system, as we discussed above. In a goal-based system, once performance reaches a specified level (the goal) a financial incentive of fixed size is awarded. Suppose the goal was a customer satisfaction rate of 95% for the month. If the person or unit reached or exceeded 95%, the financial award would be added to the salary for that month. In contrast, a continuous improvement incentive system gives larger and larger financial incentives for higher and higher performance. We can translate these two systems into evaluation-to-outcome connections as in Figure 11.2. The graph on the left shows evaluation-to-outcome connections for a goal-based system; the continuous improvement system is on the right.

For the goal-based system on the left, once the person gets an evaluation of +1, the goal, a financial incentive of $2,500 is given for that month. If the person is below an evaluation of +1, no incentive is given. Assuming the $2,500 is a valuable outcome, the effect of such a system is to make it very attractive for the person to get an evaluation of +1 and to make it much less attractive to get an evaluation below +1. However, as the connection graph shows us, the incentive system adds no value to getting an evaluation *above* +1. Once the goal is reached, the incentive is obtained and there is no incentive to improve further.

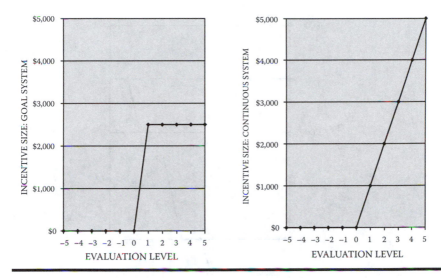

Figure 11.2. Incentive systems and evaluation-to-outcome connections.

A continuous improvement system is shown on the right. Once again, an incentive is earned for performance starting at an evaluation level of +1. The amount of the first level of incentive is lower, at $1,000, rather than the $2,500 incentive under the goal system. However, the amount of the incentive increases as performance increases. If performance reaches +2.5, the person earns an incentive equal to the goal system ($2,500). If performance is +5, an incentive of $5,000 is earned. In other words, there is value to the person to continue improving with this system.

Thus, the motivation model tells us that a goal-based system will be powerful for getting performance to +1, but not especially useful for getting performance above that level. The continuous improvement system will provide motivation to perform higher and higher above +1.

It should be very clear by now that to understand and predict motivation, we need to consider the whole model and not just a single component. In this example, other outcomes are tied to the evaluation, not just the financial incentives. High evaluations probably increase the chances for promotion, as well as levels of recognition and autonomy. They could also have important positive outcomes that are self-administered, such as feelings of accomplishment. So, we are not implying that in the goal system a person will only perform at a +1 level, then no longer try to improve beyond that. The other outcomes for higher levels of evaluation could provide the necessary motivation to perform at higher levels. What we are saying is that a goal-based *incentive system* does not increase

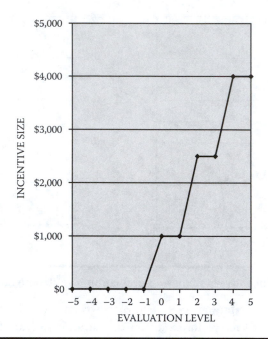

Figure 11.3. Combined goal and continuous systems.

motivation for high performance; in fact, it may actually increase motivation for performing at the *lower* +1 level.

Another option to consider is a combination of the goal and continuous improvement model. This is where there are several goal levels with increasing amounts of financial incentives awarded if the higher performance levels are reached. An example is shown in Figure 11.3. There are three goal levels, each of which has a progressively larger amount of financial incentive attached. Such a system keeps the goal level idea but allows for a broader range of performance and incentive sizes as the continuous improvement model does. So if you see an advantage to a goal-based system in your organization, using this combination approach removes some of the disadvantages of the goal-based approach.

Consistency Across People and Time

We have looked at the feedback and outcome determinants of evaluation-to-outcome connections. We now turn to the other two determinants, consistency across people and time. In predicting the effects of financial incentives, consistency across people means that everyone or every group performing at the same level receives the same level of the incentive. This is normally no problem if the measurement and the evaluation systems are good.

However, if they are not and people perceive that the measurement or evaluation systems are unfair or simply inconsistent, serious problems will result. Personnel will react with strong dissatisfaction to the incentive system and motivation will suffer. It is one thing to believe the measurement and evaluation systems are unfair. It is quite another when financial incentives are tied to this unfair system. This heightens the dissatisfaction considerably.

Another aspect of consistency across people is that everyone must have equal access to the incentives. Suppose we have a production setting where people are working on machines to produce the output. If some people have older machines based on an earlier technology, they may not be able to produce the same level of output (results) as the people on the newer machines. If incentives are tied to output, those on the faster machines will be able to get the incentives more easily than those with the slower machines. This is an example of lack of consistency across people. It can also come up when salespeople have territories which differ in expected sales levels or when consultants have client lists which produce different expected billable hours.

Consistency across time means that the rules for giving incentives must be stable over time. What usually happens with new incentive systems is that they are implemented with a measurement and evaluation system that is not that good. The flaws of these systems quickly become apparent when the incentive system is added. This results in changes being made in the incentive system rather than where the problems lie—in the measurement and/or evaluation systems.

The worst possible change is to implement the incentive system, have people start getting incentives, and then change the system so that they get less. This is deadly for satisfaction, motivation, and trust in management. Therefore, it is critical that a financial incentive system be used only when there has been a very careful analysis of the feedback system and *everyone* involved, especially the people who are in the incentive system, agrees that the feedback system is fair.

> ***Changing an installed incentive system is very***
> ***difficult. It pays to get it right the first time.***

Financial Incentives and the Outcome-to-Need Satisfaction Connection

When predicting the effects of incentives with the outcome-to-need satisfaction connections, the major issue is what makes an incentive powerful. Put in terms of the motivation model, the incentives must satisfy important needs.

Most people value money, so we are dealing with an outcome that is usually important. For the incentives to be powerful, variations in the amount of the incentive must produce large variations in expected need satisfaction. So we want unit personnel to expect that getting the incentives will be substantially more satisfying than not getting them and that getting more of the incentives will be more satisfying than getting less of them.

The motivation model tells us that if we want strong outcome-to-need satisfaction connections, the first determinant is the current need state. So at this point, will the incentives provide substantially increased need satisfaction? Remember that in evaluating outcomes, the issue is the attractiveness of a *change* in the outcome. So the question is not how important money is to subordinates, but how important an *increase* in money will be. So for the system to be powerful, the size of the incentive must be large enough to be important to people.

The conclusion that the size of the incentives must be large enough to be attractive is a rather obvious one. You did not need this book to tell you that. It is less obvious that other outcomes are tied to the incentives. The intended outcomes of recognition and achievement people get from performing well enough to get the incentives are also important. In fact, these outcomes are probably just as powerful when small financial incentives are used as when larger incentives are used. Getting the incentives means the person did a good job and the organization is recognizing that good job with the incentives. Simply making the incentives larger will not increase the outcomes of recognition or achievement. In doing your analysis, also remember that there are unintended consequences of the incentives, especially for the people who do not get them.

In addition to the need-satisfying potential of the incentives, the other determinants of the outcome-to-need satisfaction connections must be considered. We have already discussed the issue of making sure the feedback system is fair and is seen as fair. What happens when a person *expects* to receive incentives and does not get them? This is one of the unintended consequences of the incentive system and will lead to resentment. If this happens regularly, trying for the incentives will be less attractive, thereby weakening the motivating power of the incentive system. What happens when a person *compares* the size of his or her incentive with others' incentives? If the result is a feeling of unfairness or inequity, the incentive system is weakened. These effects should be considered in predicting the effects of the incentive system.

Incentives and Motivation

Based on the arguments above, we can summarize what the model predicts about implementing an incentive system. The model tells us there are a number of conditions needed for an incentive system to be effective. The more these conditions are met, the better are the chances for an effective incentive system.

- The more people there are within the unit who have a reasonable chance of getting an incentive (ability, resources, authority, and work strategies), the stronger the system will be.
- Unless people work independently, a group-based incentive system is better than an individual-based system.
- The action-to-result connections must be fairly high. People must believe they can control their results.
- A good feedback system (measurement plus evaluation) must be in place before adding financial incentives.
- All important results must be measured.
- The incentive system needs to capture the differential importance of results.
- All must agree that the measurement and evaluation systems are fair before installing the incentive system.
- Positive outcomes from the incentive system must be powerful in themselves as well as more powerful than the negative outcomes. This includes both the intended and the unintended outcomes.
- A continuous improvement incentive system is likely to be more effective than a goal-based system.
- All must agree that the planned incentive system is fair before it is installed.

What we hope is clear from this detailed discussion of incentives is that it is possible to use the model to predict the effects of interventions. It can be done with any intervention. It does take time and a careful analysis of how the intervention will influence the components of the model. It also takes a good diagnosis of the current level of the model components in the setting where the intervention is planned. However, if both the analysis and diagnosis are done carefully, the model will help you to design an optimal intervention and to predict what will happen.

Some Concluding Comments

If you have gotten this far in the book, you were clearly motivated to learn about motivation! We would like to wrap things up with a few remarks.

There was a time when managing meant telling people what to do. The job is much more complex now. You need to focus more on people. This means creating a motivating environment which produces sustainable high performance while retaining productive personnel. However, this is very difficult to do. We have tried to make it clear that motivation is complex and that understanding it takes work. Making improvements means investing considerable time and effort. With the press of all the demands on today's managers, it is easy to ignore what has to be done to create and maintain good motivation. However, our hope is that you will take the time to try what we have suggested.

While it does take work, you *can* manage motivation and manage it in a way that improves both performance and the quality of peoples' lives. If you do this, everyone benefits. The organization gets good value from your unit, you look good as a manager, your management job becomes easier, the people you supervise enjoy their work more, and our work as authors on motivation will have a positive influence on people and organizations.

We learned a great deal from writing this book. We hope you learned from it as well.

Bob Pritchard
Elissa Ashwood

Appendix 1: Our Approach to Assessing Motivation

The first author has developed a system of assessing the motivation of organizational units using the approach described in this book. The goal was to develop a cost-effective way to assess the motivation of an organizational unit in a way that would lead to identifying the strength of the connections and the determinants of these connections. The process starts with questionnaires and may include interviews as well. If you are interested in more information about this approach contact Bob Pritchard (rpritcha@pegasus.cc.ucf.edu).

Below is an example result of this process. This assessment was done with an IT unit which did complex software design for external clients. Once the data from the assessment questionnaires were collected, interviews were conducted to clarify what the improvement issues were. The conclusions in the report after each determinant are based on both the questionnaires and the interviews.

Overall Connections

The first part of the output is an assessment of the strength of each connection. Figure A1.1 shows these results for this unit.

Conclusions: Overall Connections

- Outcome-to-need satisfaction connections are good.
- Action-to-results and evaluation-to-outcome connections are moderate.
- Results-to-evaluation connections are low.

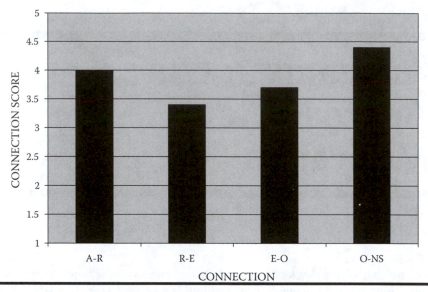

Figure A1.1. Results: Overall connections.

Determinants

The next set of results is for the determinants of each connection, shown in Figure A1.2 through Figure A1.5.

Action-to-Results Determinants

See Figure A1.2.

Conclusions: Action-to-Results Determinants

- Consider more delegation of responsibility including the authority to make decisions.
- Provide more information on tasks and project structure.
- Explore where more staff are needed.
- Consider providing training for employees for responsibilities outside of areas of formal expertise.

Results-to-Evaluation Determinants

See Figure A1.3.

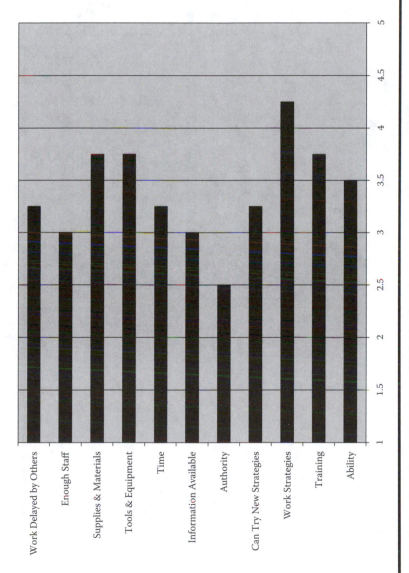

Figure A1.2. Results: Action-to-results determinants.

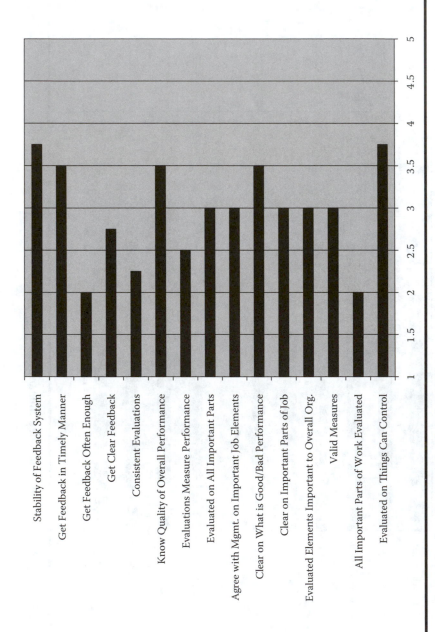

Figure A1.3. Results: Results-to-evaluation determinants.

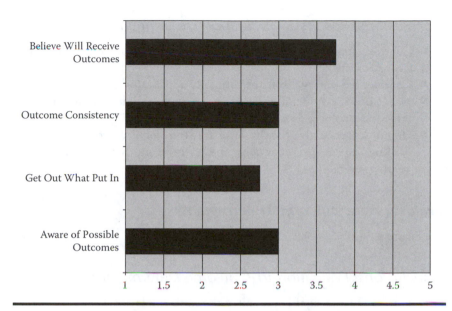

Figure A1.4.   Results: Evaluation-to-outcome determinants.

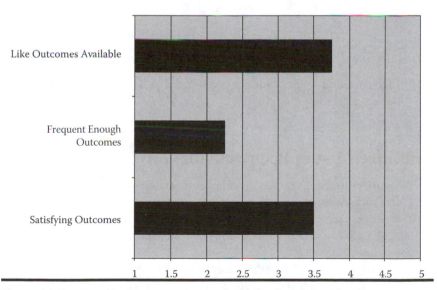

Figure A1.5.   Results: Outcome-to-need satisfaction determinants.

Conclusions: Results-to-Evaluation Determinants

- Consider starting a more regularly occurring, results-oriented, formal feedback system.
- Consider reinstating formal performance appraisals.
- Make sure any appraisal is based on a complete understanding of everything the employee does.
- Do not forget to give positive feedback, to recognize a job well done, or to recognize employees for doing the "extra" work that results from their wearing several hats.

Evaluation-to-Outcome Determinants

See Figure A1.4.

Conclusions: Evaluation-to-Outcome Determinants

- Provide more recognition for all of the work employees do.
- Carefully evaluate the consistency of the reward system.

Outcome-to-Need Satisfaction Determinants

See Figure A1.5.

Conclusions: Outcome-to-Need Satisfaction Determinants

- Problems and their solutions stem from a lack of frequent enough outcomes.

Prioritized List of Recommendations

1. Consider starting a more regularly occurring, results-oriented, formal feedback system.
2. Consider reinstating formal performance appraisals. Make sure any appraisals are based on a complete understanding of everything the employee does.
3. Do not forget to give positive feedback, to recognize a job well done, or to recognize employees for doing the "extra" work that results from their wearing several hats.
4. Provide more recognition for all of the work employees do.

5. Consider more delegation of responsibility, including authority to make decisions.
6. Clarify tasks and projects—provide more information and structure for projects.
7. Consider providing training for employees for responsibilities outside of areas of formal expertise.

Appendix 2: Drawing Connection Graphs

We noted several places in the book that your diagnosis could include drawing actual connection graphs as we do here in the book. These take some work, but can be very informative. To do this, you can model yours on the ones used in the book.

To do this, first decide what graphs to do and then what goes on the axes. Table A2.1 will help with this. To use the table, first pick the type of connection you want to do, shown in the columns in the body of the table. Then go down that column to build the graph.

For example, suppose you wanted to do an outcome-to-need satisfaction graph. As indicated by the first row under outcome-to-need satisfaction connections, you would do one for each major outcome. Typically, this would be four to six outcomes, so four to six graphs. On the horizontal axis put different levels of the each specific outcome, going from lowest to highest. Think of five to six points that would represent different levels of that outcome. For a pay raise you might use 0%, 2.5%. 5%, 7.5%, 10%, and 12.5%. Use values that are realistic in your situation. Put "anticipated satisfaction" on the vertical axis with a −10 for very dissatisfied, 0 for neutral, and +10 for very satisfied. When the axes are finished, they will look like Figure A2.1.

Then plot how satisfying each level of the outcome would be and connect the dots. It is usually easiest to start at the extremes. What would be the attractiveness of a 0% raise be? What about a 12.5% raise? Next, get the midpoint of the vertical axis. What would be the raise size that is neutral, an anticipated attractiveness value of 0. This is the raise size that is neither attractive nor unattractive.

Once you finish this, you will have three points on the graph; the attractiveness of a 0% raise, a 12.5% raise, and an attractiveness point for the raise level that is of 0 (neutral) attractiveness.

Table A2.1. Components of Connection Graphs

	Connection			
	Action-to-results	*Results-to-evaluation*	*Evaluation-to-outcome*	*Outcome-to-need-satisfaction*
Which connections?	For each result measure	For each evaluator or for each result measure/major evaluator combination	For each major outcome or each evaluator/outcome combination	For each major outcome, typically use four to six outcomes
Horizontal axis	Effort level	Result measure level	Effectiveness level	Outcome level for a single outcome
Horizontal axis scale	0 = Low to 10 = High	Amounts of a specific level of a result measure used in the action-to-results connection	−10 through 0 to +10, as used in the results-to-evaluation connection	Amounts of a single outcome, lowest realistic amount to highest realistic amount
Vertical axis	Specific levels of the result measure	Effectiveness (value to the organization)	Outcome level for a single outcome	Anticipated satisfaction (or anticipated attractiveness)
Vertical axis scale	Unacceptably low level (e.g., 10) to excellent level (e.g., 100)	−10 (unacceptably low) through 0 (minimum acceptable) to +10 (excellent)	Amounts of a single outcome, lowest realistic amount to highest realistic amount	−10 (very dissatisfied), through 0 (neutral) to +10 (very satisfied)

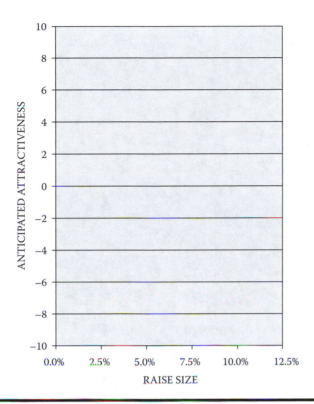

Figure A2.1. Empty outcome-to-need satisfaction graph.

To get the values between these points, ask what happens when the raise amount goes from the lowest level to the neutral level. The corresponding levels in this example are from 0% to the neutral raise. You want to decide which of three basic shapes is most accurate for this section of the curve. Is it a straight line, indicating that each improvement from 0% is of equal value? Does it stay low for raises above 0% and then rise quickly to the neutral point? As an example, this would mean that raises in the 0% to 3% range would all be about equal in attractiveness. Does it rise quickly above 0% and then level out? This would indicate a point of diminishing returns as the raise goes above 0%. Once the shape is determined to be one of these three basic shapes, draw in the actual points showing how much nonlinearity, if any, there is in this section of the curve.

Next, focus on the section of the curve from the neutral point to the maximum 12.5% raise. Again determine which of the three basic shapes best fits and how much nonlinearity, if any, exists.

Follow this process for each graph. It sounds complex, but with practice it goes fairly quickly.

References and Bibliography

Scholarly Works on Motivation

These sources are for the manager who wants to explore the research and theory base for modern motivation approaches. Most are quite academic in nature. One major exception is the work by Ed Lawler. He has been one of the best sources of academically sound work that is written for a more applied audience. We also strongly recommend the work of Gary Latham, especially his recent book on motivation.

Campbell, J. P., & Pritchard, R. D. (1976). Motivation theory in industrial and organizational psychology. In M. D. Dunnette (Ed.), *Handbook of industrial and organizational psychology* (pp. 63–130). Chicago: Rand-McNally.

Graen, G. (1969). Instrumentality theory of work motivation: Some experimental results and suggested modifications. *Journal of Applied Psychology, 53,* 1–25.

Heckhousen, H. (1991). *Motivation and action.* Berlin: Springer.

Kanfer, R. (1990). Motivation theory in industrial and organizational psychology. In M. D. Dunnette & L. M. Hough (Eds.), *Handbook of industrial and organzation psychology* (Vol. 1, 2nd ed., pp. 75–170). Palo Alto, CA: Consulting Psychologists Press.

Kanfer, R. (1992). Work motivation: New directions in theory and research. In C. L. Cooper & I. T. Robertson (Eds.), *International Review of Industrial and Organizational Psychology* (Vol. 7, pp. 1–53). London: Wiley.

Latham, G. P. (2007). *Work motivation: History, theory, research and practice.* Thousand Oaks, CA: Sage.

Latham, G. P., & Pinder, C. C. (2005). Work motivation theory and research at the dawn of the twenty-first century. *Annual Review of Psychology, 56,* 485–516.

Lawler, E. E. (1994). *Motivation in work organizations* (classic edition). San Francisco: Jossey-Bass.

Lawler, E. E., III. (2000). *Rewarding excellence.* Homewood, IL: Dorsey Press.

Lawler, E. E., III. (2001). *Organizing for high performance.* Homewood, IL: Dorsey Press.

Lawler, E. E., & Worley, C. G. (2006). *Built to change: How to achieve sustained organizational effectiveness.* San Francisco: Jossey-Bass.

Locke, E. A., & Latham, G. P. (1990). *A theory of goal-setting and task performance.* Englewood Cliffs, NJ: Prentice Hall.

Locke, E. A., & Latham, G. P. (2002). Building a practically useful theory of goal setting and task motivation: A 35-year odyssey. *American Psychologist, 57,* 705–717.

Mitchell, T. R., & Daniels, D. (2003). Motivation. In W. C. Borman, D. R. Ilgen, & R. J. Klimoski (Eds.), *Comprehensive handbook of psychology: Vol. 12. Industrial and organizational psychology.* (pp. 225–254). Hoboken, NJ: Wiley.

Naylor, J. C., Pritchard, R. D., & Ilgen, D. R. (1980). *A theory of behavior in organizations.* New York: Academic Press.

Porter, L. W., & Lawler, E. E., III. (1968). *Managerial attitudes and performance.* Homewood, IL: Dorsey Press.

Vroom, V. H. (1964). *Work and motivation.* New York: Wiley.

Designing Feedback Systems

The first article is an academic treatment of the feedback literature. The second is the first author's approach to designing and using feedback systems that fit the criteria for good feedback systems used in this book.

Kluger, A. N., & DeNisi, A. S. (1996). The effects of feedback interventions on performance: Historical review, meta-analysis, a preliminary feedback intervention theory. *Psychological Bulletin, 119,* 254–284.

Pritchard, R. D., Paquin, A. R., DeCuir, A. D., McCormick, M. J., & Bly, P. R. (2002). Measuring and improving organizational productivity: An overview of ProMES, The Productivity Measurement and Enhancement System. In R. D. Pritchard, H. Holling, F. Lammers, & B. D. Clark, (Eds.) *Improving organizational performance with the Productivity Measurement and Enhancement System: An international collaboration* (pp. 3–50). Huntington, NY: Nova Science.

Index